Doomed Edifice

Doomed Edifice

*The Eclipse of the Prophetic Ministry
and the Spiritual Captivity of the Church*

P. W. Baker

WIPF & STOCK · Eugene, Oregon

DOOMED EDIFICE
The Eclipse of the Prophetic Ministry and the Spiritual Captivity of the Church

Copyright © 2010 P. W. Baker. All rights reserved. Except for brief quotations in critical publications or reviews, no part of this book may be reproduced in any manner without prior written permission from the publisher. Write: Permissions, Wipf and Stock Publishers, 199 W. 8th Ave., Suite 3, Eugene, OR 97401.

Wipf & Stock
An Imprint of Wipf and Stock Publishers
199 W. 8th Ave., Suite 3
Eugene, OR 97401
www.wipfandstock.com

ISBN 13: 978-1-60899-040-5

Manufactured in the U.S.A.

*To: my best friend, fellow-sojourner, and wife, Stephanie
and
Claire, Chris, Sam, James, Loukas, Duncan,
Kyle, Amanda, Emma, and Judah*

*So intimate is the connection between the throne and the altar,
that the banner of the church has very seldom
been seen on the side of the people.*

—Edward Gibbon
The Decline and Fall of the Roman Empire

Contents

Acknowledgments ix
List of Abbreviations xi
Introduction xiii

1. Ecclesia 1
2. Early Organization and Worship 8
3. Early Christian Life 29
4. The Ecclesia Changes 54
5. The Rise of the Episcopacy 64
6. The Ecclesia Becomes the Church 75
7. Excursus on the Episcopacy 94
8. Excursus on the Supernatural Gifts 108
9. Recapitulation 117
10. Conclusion 123

Bibliography 135
Subject/Name Index 139

Acknowledgments

I GRATEFULLY ACKNOWLEDGE THE immeasurable debt I owe to Eberhard Arnold, Alfred Edersheim, George Edmundson, Ivan Illich, Thomas Lindsay, and Edward Selwyn—men whose writings were watersheds in my spiritual understanding and development. I recommend their works to all who seek truth above comfort.

I thank Messiah for the concurrence of circumstance that caused me to cross the path of John Clifton—who shattered forever my conceptions of the church and ministry and set me on an arduous, often uncomfortable, and yet strangely familiar, path to the truth.

I thank Valerie Severtson, my sister in the Lord, for urging me to finally write this book, and for her invaluable help in reading the manuscript, at various stages, when she had far more pressing responsibilities of family life.

My thanks also to Claire Kimball for reading the first draft and making numerous suggestions for its improvement.

Finally, I would like to thank Step for fighting with me in the struggle for truth, for her insight, and for her constant encouragement to complete the task set before me.

List of Abbreviations

1 Clem.	*1 Clement*
Did.	*Didache*
Eusebius, *Hist. eccl.*	Eusebius, *Historia ecclesiastica*
Ign. *Phld.*	Ignatius, *To the Philadelphians*
Ign. *Smyrn.*	Ignatius, *To the Smyrnaeans*
Ign. *Trall.*	Ignatius, *To the Trallians*
Irenaeus, *Haer.*	Irenaeus, *Against Heresies*
Justin, *1 Apol.*	Justin, *Apologia i*
Minucius Felix, *Oct.*	Minucius Felix, *Octavius*
Origen, *Cels.*	Origen, *Contra Celsum*
Rom. Hist.	*Roman History*
Tacitus, *Ann.*	Tacitus, *Annales*

Introduction

IF THE COMINGLING OF Christianity and politics in the United States for the past thirty years is representative, apparently Christian doctrine now includes being patriotic and supporting the troops, being against abortion, for gun ownership, against homosexuality, against welfare, for the death penalty, and for free-market capitalism. But those defining qualities denote a particularly American political viewpoint and agenda that has virtually nothing to do with historic Christianity. In fact, it is safe to say that first century Christians would concur with only two items on that list—homosexuality and abortion. Yet, to the believers of that time, those two sins were understood as manifestations of all sinful sexual behavior and killing of any kind. So, quite simply, American Christianity has got it wrong.

It must be admitted that few who call themselves Christians today are either aware of or care about this play-acting that passes for living as a disciple of Messiah Jesus. And it is neither an exaggeration nor cynical to say that many evangelical Christians in the United States believe that Jesus came into the world and died so that all people would be guaranteed life, liberty, and the pursuit of happiness.

Yet, it's not only American, evangelical, fundamental, reformed, charismatic, Bible-based Christianity that has got it wrong. All institutional Christianity has strayed from its original path and created a host of convenient excuses that permit a way of life that is contrary to its earliest doctrines and principles. What is surprising is how quickly it began to stray.

No single event brought Christianity to its current lamentable state. Rather, a confluence of decisions in the first and second centuries—decisions deemed both justified and prudent by those who made them—produced the institutional Christianity, the church that exists today. Once those decisions were implemented and established, inertia prevailed. Over the ensuing centuries, a few lonely souls howled for restoration, but it was far easier to dispatch those who howled than attempt to recover whatever was lost. Anyway, inertia had its emoluments—and it's extremely difficult to compete with emoluments.

But the church paid an awful price.

Before Israel went in to take possession of the land given to them by Jehovah, Moses explained repeatedly that they were being given the land not because they were more righteous, but that the current inhabitants of that land were being dispossessed as punishment for their sin (Deut 9:4–6). Israel was being used by Jehovah as an instrument of wrath. Moses carefully instructed Israel that they were to make no treaties with the nations residing there (Deut 7:2), or covet their gold (Deut 7:25), or intermarry with them (Deut 7:3–4), but to drive them out entirely. He warned that, if Israel comingled with the surrounding cultures, they would be snared into serving other gods and Jehovah would also remove them from the land (Deut 4:23–28).

It's amazing how quickly everything deteriorated.[1] The events are recorded in the first two chapters of Judges. Joshua brought the tribes across the Jordan and into the land. Judah, Ephraim, and Manasseh only partially drove out the inhabitants from their allotted portions. The rest of the tribes did not drive out those who inhabited the remaining allotments. Thus, the Angel of the Lord walked among them and announced judgment (Judg 2:1–3). Those who had experienced Jehovah's awesome power and protection during the exodus from Egypt were spared from witnessing the apostasy and disaster to follow (Judg 2:7–13).

Israel eventually comingled with the native cultures and served their gods. Jehovah sent prophets to call them to repentance, but Israel ignored them, or prohibited them from speaking, or killed them. After repeated pleadings and numerous warnings, Jehovah removed Israel from the land and sent them into captivity. Those he chose—"the pupil of his eye"— were banished from their inheritance. Yet, Jehovah didn't forget them. He hid and recalled a remnant many decades later, eventually bringing forth Messiah through that remnant for the sake of all mankind.

Scripture contains many lessons that are woven like threads through both its Testaments. One of those threads is that deliberate and unrepentant sin, especially by those whom Jehovah has chosen, results in captivity and exile for that individual or group, and serves as both punishment and

---

1. Israel's willful sin started much earlier, of course—long before they entered the land: Korah's rebellion and the Baal of Peor incident, to name only two examples.

an impetus to repentance. Just so, Israel's apostasy and subsequent captivity has always been a clear, prophetic message for the church.

Thirty years ago, near the end of summer, and shortly before I was to start seminary classes, I met a young man whom I later discovered was an apostle. We met while I was working part-time at the publishing warehouse where he worked. He was a voracious reader and had an astonishing memory (he could recite huge portions of Scripture and was a human concordance), spent his lunch hour in prayer (perched twenty feet up on the stacks of boxed books in the warehouse), loved science fiction, and was actually fun to be with. He was one of several pastors of a small church that met in the rented basement of a post office in a nearby town.

Over the following weeks, we discussed some of the concerns I had since reading *Deschooling Society* earlier that summer. I was having second thoughts about the validity of the church as an institution and the establishment of an ordained class of leaders, and was also skeptical that the institutional church was actually the church that Jesus established.

He wanted to help me sort things out and suggested that I read *The Church and the Ministry in the Early Centuries* by Thomas Lindsay and *The Problem of Wineskins* by Howard Snyder. He predicted somewhat ominously that the Lord would take it from there.

He was correct. Those two books led to more questions and many more books, years of frustration and impatience, and much prayer. Although it took far longer than I expected, what finally emerged was a radical concept of the state of the church—but it is not a novel idea.

Twenty-five years or so before the outbreak of the First World War, biblical scholars in Europe, Great Britain, and the United States were engaged in a vigorous debate over first- and second-century church polity and doctrine. Those men are all dead and their books are in danger of being forgotten—abandoned in dark recesses of university libraries or used book stores. But their meticulous research and clear insight remain relevant and instructive.

Edward Selwyn—one of those scholars—wrote: "True criticism is really constructive in its tendency. When it seems to destroy, it is only removing materials from a doomed edifice to build a new and more enduring dwelling."[2] That is the goal of this survey. It is not a purist's ir-

---

2. Selwyn, *St. Luke the Prophet*, 6.

rational devotion to an abstract principle, but a practical critique in the hope of recalling something more truthful and enduring—a digest and synthesis of the historic record that explains the wantonness, horror, and play-acting that is both the past and current state of the church. As is the case with any analysis leading to judgment, it does not examine all details, but selects and sifts for those "significant in relation to the point at issue."[3] It is too easy to get entangled by all the intricacies of history and miss the bigger lessons it can teach us.

Adolf Deissmann explains that the words of Jesus were not recorded for posterity in their original Aramaic because "Christianity, in becoming a world religion, gradually forgot its oldest records—records that had originated far away from the world and were unintelligible to the world—and so they were lost."[4] It is intriguing that Deissmann's explanation applies to far more than merely the language chosen for the New Testament documents. The church forgot and lost a great many things.

Thirty years ago, I wondered if the institutional Christian Church was actually the same church that Jesus established. As we examine various events from the first three centuries of church history, the answer to that question will be evident. But something of far greater significance will become evident—something that has not been hidden and is hardly esoteric. It has been evident for nearly two thousand years: the institutional church is an edifice built upon man's wisdom and was doomed to failure. How this occurred and what it means to all who call on the name of the Lord Jesus follows.

The events we examine may disturb what you thought was settled history. But, disturbed or not, we must all give an accounting.

---

3. Dewey, 122.
4. Deissmann, 57–58.

1

Ecclesia

Before we examine the lives of the early believers and the organization and worship of the early church, we need to take a moment to consider what we mean by the word *church*.

Words are icons or symbols for expressing thought. They stand in place of something else—a concept or a thing, either real or imaginary. But words have only the meaning that we impose on them—or, simply put: "words don't mean, people mean."[1] We express thought and communicate adequately only by tacit agreement on a word's meaning. So, what a word means—and what we mean when we use a word—is crucial, since a word can mean different things to different people.

Semantics is the study of meaning in communication—which is more than the mere definition of words. In semantics, the *denotation* of a word is that thing we can point to when we use that word.[2] The *connotation* of a word is the emotional content, the feeling, or the mental images that word brings to mind. What we refer to as the *meaning* of a word is the *combination of its denotation and connotation*.

It is clear that words often survive for extended periods of time, yet take on an entirely different meaning, long after their original meaning has vanished or been forgotten.[3] If I use a word's older meaning in conversation with someone who is unaware of it, I will almost certainly fail to communicate what I intended—all of which brings us to the word *church*.

---

1. Salomon, 2. Salomon's work is a concise introduction to semantics.

2. Some words do not have an observable denotation. For example: truth, beauty, honesty. These are known as vague or abstract terms.

3. Those interested should consult Richard Trench's work, listed in the bibliography.

The word *church* is derived from the Greek word *kuriaké*, "signifying the Lord's, or belonging to the Lord."[4] When we use the word *church* in everyday conversation, we are usually denoting both the building where a group of Christians meet[5] and the people in that building. Connotations, by their nature, vary by individual, by denomination, and even by culture, but might include a pastor and elders, prayer books, hymnals, organ music, choirs, stained glass, a steeple, a quiet or sacred retreat from the world, and so on. All of this—the denotation and connotation combined—is generally what we mean when we use the word church in conversation *today*. Yet, because the word church has survived for an extended period of history, and since our study concerns the *early* church, we need to make certain we avoid imputing meaning to the word church that did it not possess originally.

Edwin Hatch and Fenton Hort also faced this problem in their two studies of the early church. Referring to the word *church*, Hatch says, "we tend almost inevitably to carry back with us into the past times those conceptions of it which we have derived from our modern experience."[6] That is, we unintentionally impute both the denotation and connotation of the institution's current or modern form upon its earliest form. "By the slow and silent alchemy of time," Hatch continues, "institutions change: but, while institutions change, the words which designate them frequently remain permanent. We consequently tend to make the more or less unconscious assumption that the same word designated in past times what it designates now."[7]

Hort goes so far as to completely abandon the word *church* in his study, preferring instead to use the word *ecclesia*[8]—the Greek word that is translated *church* in our English Bibles. He writes: "The English term *church*, now the most familiar representative of *ecclesia* to most of us, carries with it associations derived from the institutions and doctrines of later times, and thus cannot at present without a constant mental effort be made to convey the full and exact force which originally belonged to *ecclesia*. . . . *Ecclesia* is the only perfectly colourless word within reach,

---

4. MacLeod, 1.
5. Jews meet in a synagogue, Muslims in a mosque.
6. Hatch, 15.
7. Ibid., 15.
8. The transliteration of ἐκκλησία may also be written as *ekklesia*.

carrying us back to the beginnings of Christian history, and enabling us in some degree to get behind words and names to the simple facts which they originally denoted."[9]

Hatch and Hort both warn of what we will call an illegitimate transfer of meaning. Without constant attention, it's possible to commit illegitimate transfer of meaning on the word church as it existed and was experienced by early Christians. And, since Hort also states that the word church "carries with it association derived from the . . . doctrines of later time," it is equally possible to commit an "illegitimate transfer of doctrine" as well.

Since our goal is to "get behind words and names to the simple facts," we'll examine how the early Christians understood both the church—its organization and doctrine—and themselves as believers. Then we can compare the organization and doctrine of the early church with the contemporary Western church.

Hort prefers the term *ecclesia* because it is perfectly colorless. But, *congregation* and *assembly* are equally colorless words, and for the same reason. Like *ecclesia*, *congregation* and *assembly* do not necessarily possess religious connotations. So, in order to avoid the pitfalls Hatch and Hort describe, let's substitute *ecclesia* (or its plural form *ecclesiae*), *congregation*, or *assembly* when referring to the gathering of early Christians. We'll restrict the term *church* to the institutional form of the ecclesia that developed in the fourth century—as we shall see.[10]

THE WORD *ECCLESIA*

When Jesus established his ecclesia upon the confession of Peter[11] within the pagan territory near Caesarea-Philippi—a city where Augustus was

---

9. Hort, 1–2.

10. The expression "primitive Christianity" is frequently encountered in histories of the early church. But it is has pejorative connotations and implies that the early believers were not so evolved or enlightened as we are—which remains to be seen.

11. Lindsay, 6 n 1. It is Peter's acknowledgment of who Jesus is that is the foundation of the church. Lowrie notes: "But that this power was bestowed upon [Peter] in his official capacity as apostle (or as chief of the apostles), there is no hint,—still less that it was an official prerogative which was meant to descend to an individual successor of Peter in the primacy of the Church (according to the Roman view), or to the bishops as representatives in solidum of the episcopate of Peter (according to the doctrine of Cyprian). On the contrary, we see from John 20:22, 23, and Matt. 18:17–20 that this power is given to the disciples as such and to the Church as a whole:—to every one that confesses a like

worshipped as a god in a temple built and dedicated to him by Herod Philip[12]—he chose a word that was already rich in history and connotation for both Jew and gentile.[13] Both understood *ecclesia* to mean primarily "assembly." To the Jew, the ecclesia was the solemn assembly of Israel. To the gentile, it was the formal assembly of citizens in the Greek city-state. Both assemblies were convened by the blowing of a trumpet. In evangelical circles today, it is a common, but mistaken, notion that *ecclesia* means those "called out," implying that Christians are called out from the world. But the "calling out" element of the word refers to people being *called out from their houses* by the herald's trumpet.[14]

As noted above, *ecclesia* is not primarily a religious term. Luke, for example, uses *ecclesia* in its nonreligious sense to describe the tumultuous assembly at the amphitheater in Ephesus (Acts 19:32, 39).[15] However, as Jesus and his apostles used *ecclesia*, the most important antecedent meaning was its religious sense.[16] *Ecclesia* expresses an idea that had its roots in the old, yet foretold the future.[17] When Jesus expressed the idea of ecclesia[18] to his disciples, they understood he meant "the congregation of God." Jesus was saying that he was building *his* Israel—the Ecclesia of Messiah. It would be the old in new form[19]—new wine in new wineskins. Paul certainly understood this. In his parting address at Miletus (Acts 20:28), Paul substitutes *ecclesia* for the Hebrew word ʽ*ēdhāh* in the Old Testament passage he cites (Ps 74:2), and thus facilitates the use of *ecclesia* for "the people of God."[20]

The Twelve became that first little ecclesia—the rock upon which an ever-enlarging ecclesia would be built, stone by living stone.[21] Its

---

faith with Peter, and, as a living stone, is built into the same edifice." Lowrie, *The Church and its Organization*, 123.

12. Lindsay, 3.
13. Ibid., 4.
14. Lindsay, 4–5; Hort, 5–6.
15. Hort, 97.
16. Ibid., 8.
17. Lindsay, 5.
18. It is unimportant which word Jesus actually used when he spoke to the disciples, since the writers of the New Testament chose to use *ecclesia*.
19. Hort, 11.
20. Ibid., 13–14.
21. Ibid., 17.

foundation would be the Twelve, then—like concentric circles—widen to Jerusalem, to Samaria, to Galilee, Antioch, Asia, Rome, Europe, and the world. It was the Ecclesia of Messiah, and the Twelve were what the ecclesia was to be always: faith in and devotion to the Lord Jesus—union and brotherly love.[22]

In *The Church and the Ministry in the Early Centuries*, Thomas Lindsay lists five characteristics of the ecclesia: (1) *fellowship*, (2) *unity*, (3) *visible community*, (4) *authority*, and (5) *sacerdotal society*.[23] From its inception, the ecclesia was a divine *fellowship* with the Messiah and with the members of the community. It was a reality, but more ideal than material.[24] The ecclesia was a *unity* (Eph 4:3–6) that "had thrown down all walls of sex, race, and social usages which have kept men separate."[25] Although Christian unity is a primary truth, it is a religious experience—never an earthly throne. It is heavenly, yet under dominion of Messiah. Each society, each congregation, was *the* body of Messiah—not *part* of the body of Messiah.[26] The ecclesia was a *visible community* to the world, just as Israel had been a visible community—surrounded by the world, yet distinct and separate from it. The ecclesia possessed *authority*. It was democratic, in that all members possessed authority, yet it was a theocracy, in that Messiah ruled over it. Jesus transferred the "keys"—the rabbinic authority to bind and loose—to Peter, to the Twelve, and to all believers down through time. And, finally, the ecclesia was a *sacerdotal society*—its members offering their bodies, praise, almsgiving, good deeds, and service in sacrifice.[27] In addition to Lindsay's five characteristics, Hort has compiled eleven classes of how the word *ecclesia* is used in the New Testament.[28]

22. Ibid., 20.
23. Lindsay, 6–37.
24. Ibid., 13.
25. Ibid., 12.
26. Ibid., 14.
27. Ibid., 34.
28. Hort's eleven classes of usage are: (1) the original ecclesia of Jerusalem or Judaea, at a time when there was no other; (2) the single local ecclesia of a city, which is named; (3) the individual ecclesia addressed, or in one case the ecclesia of the city from which the epistle was written; (4) any individual ecclesia; (5) the sum of individual ecclesiae in a named region; (6) ecclesia not of a definite region, nor yet the sum of all individual ecclesia; (7) the sum of all individual ecclesiae or all but the one written to; (8) the one universal ecclesia as represented in the local individual ecclesia, as in the address to the Ephesian elders; (9) the one universal ecclesia absolutely—this is confined to the twin

Jesus originally established his ecclesia as an independent, self-governing theocracy in the midst of pagan society. He designated it *his* ecclesia—singular—meaning all believers throughout the ages. As the gospel spread over the Roman Empire, Paul and the other apostles established small, independent, self-governing congregations—each one an ecclesia. They were indeed part of the larger ecclesia, but each was an ecclesia unto itself—an independent, self-governing theocracy.[29] Jesus guided these assemblies by the Holy Spirit and bound them together through the prophetic ministry—the apostles and prophets.

The ecclesia was not *a* body of Christ, not *part of* the body of Christ, but *the* body of Christ.[30] It is noteworthy that in 100 of the 110 instances where ecclesia is used in the New Testament, it denotes the local, independent assembly of believers.[31] Paul addresses the Ephesian elders at Miletus as an independent ecclesia—indeed part of the universal ecclesia, but also an insular society.[32] Yet, he encourages the ecclesia at Corinth to consider itself as united to "all who in every place invoke the name of our Lord Jesus Christ."[33] We see the individuality of the local ecclesiae and, at the same time, Paul taking great pains to "counteract any tendency towards isolation and wantonness of independence, which might arise in the young communities which he founded, or with which he came in contact."[34] Thus, each ecclesia was both a partial society and a unity of its own. Each congregation determined its own activities. The ecclesia at Antioch, for example, was never charged with exceeding its legitimate power in sending forth Paul and Barnabas.[35]

Members of the ecclesia of Israel had been holy by fact of membership,[36] and the Christian ecclesiae adopted this concept quickly.

---

epistles to Ephesians and Colossians; (10) what may be called a domestic ecclesia; and (11) an assembly of an ecclesia, rather than the ecclesia itself. In each case, Hort cites examples, which I have not reproduced. See Hort, 116–18.

29. Lindsay, 20, 25, 33, 177.
30. Ibid., 14.
31. Ibid., 10.
32. Hort, 103.
33. Ibid., 119.
34. Ibid.
35. Ibid., 67.
36. Ibid., 56.

But, as Walter Lowrie notes, our Western conception of membership is far different from that of the early ecclesia:

> The primitive notion was that every "brother" when once he was recognized as such, was to be accounted a member in any Church where he might happen to be. St. Paul, as soon as he was known to be a Christian, was recognized as a member of the Church in Jerusalem, he was welcomed by the Church in Antioch, and, of course, by every church of his own founding. Nor did he cease to be a member of one when he became a member of another.... When he was absent from Corinth in the body but desired to exercise authority there he pleads that he is "present in spirit" and "as present" pronounces his judgment.... Being in Asia, he was still a member of the Church in Corinth,—he was a member at the same time of many Churches, of all the Churches, because he was a member of the Church universal, of which every local church is a manifestation.... It was merely a question of recognition not of enrollment in this or that local congregation.[37]

By conceiving membership in this way, early believers were able to grasp the idea of the universal ecclesia. The ecclesiae were encouraged to think of their own congregation as part of the larger ecclesia of all believers, but it was always more sentiment than reality.[38] The ideal Ecclesia of Messiah would become a reality only at Jesus' return, at the restoration of all things. Even though congregations were part of a larger group, their independence was always primary.

The idea of these various ecclesiae as independent theocracies—tiny islands "in a sea of surrounding paganism"[39]—was evident in the way they organized themselves as well. Although no hierarchy existed in those early congregations, the contrast to the institutional church today extends far beyond a simple organizational structure.

---

37. Lowrie, *Problems of Church Unity*, 34–35.
38. Lindsay, 199.
39. Ibid., 57.

2

Early Organization and Worship

THE NEW TESTAMENT DOES not specify, nor did the apostles dictate, a particular form of government for the ecclesiae. From the earliest days, the congregations organized themselves in a variety of forms—some of which were adapted from the surrounding Roman society.[1]

The congregations, says Lindsay, "were well acquainted with social organization of various kinds, which entered into their daily life in the world."[2] The ecclesiae selectively incorporated, specialized, and adapted for their own use various elements of the social organizations that already existed in the Roman society around them.

Christian terminology was also extracted from common speech—"extracted and specialized for Christian purposes."[3] For example, the word *bishop* was borrowed directly from the Greek secular associations, where either *bishop* (ἐπίσκοπος) or *finance officer* (ἐπιμελητής) was the title given to the overseer or treasurer responsible for investing the funds of the society and deciding upon their distribution. Private institutions and municipalities throughout the Roman Empire employed both bishops and finance officers for this office, and their importance would easily have transferred to the ecclesia, since charitable work was a prominent aspect of community life.[4]

Lindsay has determined five basic types, or models, of organization in the early congregations. Each was adapted by the various Christian assemblies. They were (1) "the Seven," (2) the Jerusalem congregation, (3)

---

1. Hatch, 213.
2. Lindsay, 114.
3. Wotherspoon, 120.
4. Hatch, 36–37.

the client-patron relationship, (4) confraternities (*collegiae*), and (5) the synagogue.

The first attempt at organization—"the Seven"—occurs when the "service of tables" is set apart from the larger body of believers (Acts 6:1–6). It was a simple division of responsibility of service to the congregation. Unlike Western notions that imply service is second-rate or the lowest form of work, Lindsay notes the highest administrative position the church could bestow was the "ministry of the tables."

> Unless we are to believe that the appointment of the *seven* was a merely temporary expedient, it is only natural to suppose that the duty of distributing money and other gifts among the poor was performed by the men who were appointed by the Church to do it, or by others appointed in the same way and for the same purpose; and the natural inference is that the *Seven* of Acts 6 were the *elders* of Acts 11. . . . They are never called *deacons*; the *Seven* is the technical name they were known by. . . . This earliest example of Christian ecclesiastical organization contains in it three interesting elements—apostolic guidance and sanction; the self-government and independence of the community evinced in the responsibility for good government laid upon the whole membership; and, as a result, a representative system of administration suggested by the everyday surroundings of the people.[5]

The second type—the Jerusalem congregation—was structured along blood lines, with James, the Lord's brother, at its head.[6] The historian Eusebius records that, after the death of James, the remaining members of the ecclesia at Jerusalem met and selected Symeon, the son of the Lord's paternal uncle, to lead the ecclesia (*Hist. eccl.* 3.11.1–2). In the fifteenth year of Emperor Domitian (96 CE), the grandsons of the Lord's brother, Judas, were dragged before the emperor and contemptuously returned to Judea, after it was clear they posed no threat.[7] The Jerusalem congregation continued to promote blood relatives to this position until well into the reign of Trajan (98–117 CE). This type of organization around a blood line has no counterpart elsewhere in the New Testament.[8]

---

5. Lindsay, 116–18.
6. Ibid., 119–20.
7. Ibid., 120.
8. Ibid., 120–21.

At Derbe, Lystra, and Iconium, Paul and Barnabas left behind them communities of Christians with elders at their head—the apostles "*appointed* for them elders in every church" (Acts 14:23). The word *appointed* (χειροτονήσαντες) means "strictly, to elect by popular vote" and suggests that Paul and Barnabas followed the example of the Jerusalem congregation, by superintending an election of office-bearers. The title *elders* (πρεσβύτεροι) was probably derived from the Jerusalem ecclesia.[9]

Other congregations were organized like the client-patron relationship, a social organization that existed widely in the Roman world, but which has no analogue in contemporary Western culture. When the ecclesiae adapted this model, the wealthy members of the congregation opened their homes and shared their material blessings, thereby taking on the patron aspect, while the remaining members took on the role of the clients. Arrangements like these were so common in secular Roman society that it permitted the Christians to hide for years in its shadow. In his letters to the Romans (Rom 12:8) and Thessalonians (1 Thess 5:12), Paul calls these leaders "those who are over you in the Lord," choosing a term (προϊστήμι) that suggests a special relationship between the leaders and the led—namely, the client-patron relationship familiar to Roman society.[10]

Lindsay notes, "The infant Christian churches came into being in the Greco-Roman world at a time when the imperial policy was extremely jealous of any form of social organization, and when its officials were on the watch to prevent any new development of the principle."[11] Any illegal or suspicious assembly could be suppressed without warning. In spite of this danger, some ecclesiae were organized with elements taken from the confraternities (*collegiae*), which existed widely among the various religions and trades. Even though they were periodically restricted or outlawed, confraternities flourished throughout the empire and provided the fourth model for Christian congregations. Burial societies—one such *collegium*—ensured that the funeral plans of its members would be carried out at death. Most confraternities afforded a regular opportunity for their members to gather in a convivial atmosphere over a common meal.

Christians also met together for a common meal. And, because of their external resemblance to the confraternities, Tertullian (160–220 CE)

---

9. Ibid., 118.
10. Ibid., 123.
11. Ibid., 132.

argued that the ecclesiae should be recognized as a legal association. Yet Pliny, the Roman governor of Bithynia-Pontus (111–13 CE), believed he was legally justified in proceeding against Christians as members of an *illicit collegium*.[12] Confraternities were extensive, incorporating diverse political and social interests and the various trades. Many Christians had been members of confraternities prior to conversion. Some even retained their membership after conversion—originally when conscience permitted, but also later, when they had to be cajoled into dissociating from them.[13]

The synagogue supplied the fifth ecclesiastical model, especially for Jewish converts. Apart from the temple at Jerusalem, the synagogue was the center of what it meant to be a Jew. Historians and scholars assume that it originated during the captivity in Babylon—the Jews bringing it back with them when they returned. By the first century, synagogues were established widely in most of the larger cities of the Roman Empire. Since many of the earliest Christian converts were Jews, it was natural for them to form Christian congregations based on the synagogue. It offered the comfort of tradition, especially when separated from fellow Jews who did not acknowledge Jesus as Messiah. Ecclesiae based on the synagogue were naturally more structured in leadership than the Gentile models. And because Judaism was a *religio licita* (protected religion) in the empire, the Christian assemblies were, for a time, able to avoid attention if they appeared as merely another synagogue. Though this model became scarce after the destruction of Jerusalem in 70 CE, it did not vanish entirely.[14]

These models were not copied slavishly or mechanically. Instead, elements were selectively adapted for use at the discretion of the individual congregations. No evidence exists of a single acceptable organizational model for the Christian congregations. The apostles did not impose any particular structure on the congregations. Instead, they left each congregation free to decide its form as an independent ecclesia. "There is a Visible Catholic Church of Christ," says Lindsay, "consisting of all those throughout the world who visibly worship the same God and Father, profess their faith in the same Saviour, and are taught by the same Holy Spirit; but I do not see any Scriptural or even primitive warrant for insisting that catholicity *must* find visible expression in a uniformity of organization, of

---

12. Ibid., 135.
13. Ibid., 127.
14. For a full discussion of these five models, see Lindsay, 117–30.

ritual of worship, or even of formulated creed." There is no "one method of selecting and setting apart office-bearers who rule the Church."[15]

It is only later, and gradually, that structure is imposed upon the congregations.

THE PROPHETIC MINISTRY

Prophecy is an essential ingredient of religion. In the first century, oracles of every kind were held in awe by the common man. Of the six major oracles at that time, none was more trustworthy than the Delphic oracle—Pythian Apollo.[16] Consultants who could afford the journey and the requisite offerings sought "aid and light in matters of public and private import."[17] While most of the intellectuals of that age scoffed, Plutarch recognized that there was a supernatural force behind the Delphic oracle, even if he ascribed it to demons.[18] At Delphi, the Pythia ascended a tripod erected over what once had been a deep crevice in the rocky earth. From there, in a mantic state, she spoke to her prophet (προφήτης), who stood nearby and translated the Pythia's ambiguous utterances to the consultant.

When the Roman emperor Julian attempted to revive paganism in the fourth century and sought guidance in his effort, Delphic Apollo pronounced its own demise. "Tell the King," said the Pythia, ". . . the speaking water is quenched." This was the last oracle spoken at Delphi. After Julian's death, the emperor Theodosius closed the temple, and his son and successor, Arcadius, had it demolished.[19]

Numerous lesser oracles wandered about the empire. As Lindsay points out, "professional prophets and priests of Syrian, Persian, and perhaps of Indian cults, passed along the high-roads."[20] Paul and Silas encountered a pythia while in Philippi (Acts 16:16–18). But the Christian prophets had nothing in common with these pagan oracles. The Christian prophets provided leadership to the ecclesiae, strengthened, and bound

---

15. Lindsay, viii–ix.
16. Dempsey, 81.
17. Ibid., 82.
18. Ibid., 72.
19. Ibid., 180–81.
20. Lindsay, 101.

them together. They formed the nucleus of the ecclesia of Messiah. Around them were gathered the first elements of Christianity.[21]

The earliest description of leadership in the ecclesia is a twofold division of the *prophetic ministry* and the *local ministry*. The prophetic ministry—or the "ministry of the Word"—consisted of the apostles and prophets, whom Paul calls the foundation of the ecclesia (Eph 2:20). The prophetic ministry was like the prophetic office of the Old Testament, except that it was more widespread. New Testament prophets were no more automatically part of the local ministry than Old Testament prophets were automatically part of the priesthood.[22] And just as there was lack of discernment on the part of Israel in the Old Testament, eventually there was lack of discernment, subsequent deterioration, and the introduction of false doctrine into the early Christian congregations.[23] The local ministry—or the "ministry of tables"—consisted of the pastors, teachers, elders, and deacons. But these two divisions were not mutually exclusive—a believer could be several or all of them.[24] However, the prophetic ministry was the more esteemed of the two.

The distinction between prophet and apostle[25] is often misunderstood.

> It was the apostolate in its widest extent that was a part of the "prophetic ministry" of the primitive Church. When we think of apostles as part of the triad of "apostles, prophets and teachers," we

---

21. Selwyn, *The Christian Prophets*, viii.
22. Lindsay, 108.
23. Ibid., 108.
24. Ibid., 65–66.
25. The word *apostle* (ἀπόστολος, *apostolos*) appears eighty times in the New Testament. It may be translated *apostle, emissary, messenger,* or *delegate*—one sent on behalf of another. Like *ecclesia*, *apostolos* is not primarily a religious term. Although it calls to mind for us a select group of authoritative delegates (the Twelve, Paul, Barnabas, etc.), the word itself was not understood that way by the early ecclesiae. As Selwyn and Lindsay both note, apostles were commissioned by the congregations themselves as needs arose for their work or at the direction of the Holy Spirit. In light of this, it is curious that many translations (ASV, KJV, NKJV, NASB, and ESV) attempt to force a distinction in 2 Cor 8:23 and Phlm 2:25, where *apostolos* is translated "messenger" instead of "apostle." Louw and Nida concur with this distinction. It is doubtful, however, that translating *apostolos* as *messenger* in these instances can be honestly maintained. What seems more likely is that, by translating it *messenger*, a subtle attempt is made to restrict the apostolate to a select few. No such distinction or nuance existed in the congregations of the first century—until the emergence of the theory of apostolic succession, which we will examine later.

must have in mind, not twelve or thirteen, but large numbers who were missionaries in the Church, and took the first rank in the prophetic ministry because their duty was to extend the boundaries of the Church of Christ. They all belonged to the class of those "gifted" to "speak the Word of God," men who were to be tested by the discriminating "gift," but who, when received, were to be honoured and their word obeyed. The spiritual "gift" which they possessed was a personal and not an official thing; and in one sense they were all on the same level, for they had all the same "gift." But they differed in natural endowments, and the spiritual gift had been bestowed in larger measure on some than on others. Some could, and did, fill a large sphere and wield an enormous influence; others had to content themselves with a much inferior position; but whether their sphere was large or small they had the same work to do. They were the pioneers of primitive Christianity. They cannot be compared with the officials of a long established church. The only safe comparison is with the missionary of modern times, and their work has the curious double action which must characterize pioneer Christian work in all places and at all times.

They had to teach Christian morality to converts ignorant of its first principles, and this could only be done when stern command mingled with sweet persuasiveness. They had to deal with people who could but awkwardly apply the moral principles they had been taught, and had to select typical cases, and to point out how they must be decided. On the one side their action must appear to be highly autocratic; on the other their influence was entirely personal, and their only means of enforcing their decisions was by persuasion.[26]

Selwyn explains further that the apostle and prophet were merely two aspects of the same gift or commission:

Whereas "the Apostle" was the term used in connection with the movements on Circuit, the term used of the same person when speaking or preaching is "the Prophet." . . . Each one who was *sent forth* on a mission of the Gospel, including Jesus Himself, was so far forth an Apostle: that is purely a grammatical necessity, for grammar makes the word Apostle the verbal substantive of the Greek word "to send forth." If the mission was often repeated, the person so sent would undoubtedly become entitled to the name Apostle. That every Apostle was also a Prophet, without exception, is a statement which has the highest degree of probability; for

---

26. Lindsay, 85–86.

the special errands on which simple messengers were sent forth would probably not be repeated, and thus the title Apostle would not attach permanently to simple messengers, as it would attach to Prophets.

The above remarks point to the conclusion that a Prophet on his circuit was an Apostle. . . . Elders were Prophets, and Prophets were Elders, in New Testament times. And it cannot be denied that Elders were frequently Apostles.[27]

Sewlyn describes the process whereby prophets became apostles:

> The Prophets were sometimes sent upon circuits or Missionary Journeys, and when so sent forth they became Apostles. After going on Circuit frequently they would naturally become known as Apostles, and would take precedence of Prophets who had not been so sent forth.[28]

The work of prophets and apostles can further be differentiated from the work of evangelists, in that "Prophets are those who receive Apocalypses, Apostles are those Prophets who go on Missionary journeys, Evangelists are those who preach the Gospel without being Prophets, though they go on Missions.[29]"

Lindsay notes that

> . . . wandering prophets might easily become apostles and we can see an example of this change of work when Barnabas, who did a prophet's work in Antioch, was, at the call of the Spirit, sent, along with Saul, to undertake the work of an apostle or missionary in Cyprus, Pamphylia, Pisidia and Lycaonia. When these wandering prophets settled down for a time with their families, in any Christian community, far from home and employment, it was but right that the community they benefited by their labours should support them.[30]

Charles Gore stresses the conscious activity of the prophet:

> In marked contrast to the idea of a prophet in Plato and in Philo, St. Paul insists that the Christian prophet is no unconscious, passive instrument of the Spirit. Prophecy is rational, and subject to

---

27. Selwyn, *St. Luke the Prophet*, 28, 31–32.
28. Ibid., 248.
29. Ibid., 202n.
30. Lindsay, 98.

the will of the prophet in a remarkable manner; see 1 Cor xiv. and especially verse 32 : "the spirits of the prophets" (cf. Apoc. xxii.6) "are subject to the prophets", also Rom. xii. 6, and Acts xxi. 4, 11, where St. Paul seems to regard prophetic utterances as misdirected in intention though true in fact.... The Christian prophet is no individual oracle. He is one of a body, and his gift exists for the good of the whole body. Accordingly it is subordinated to the regulative authority in the body, in the interest of order: see 1 Cor. xii. and xiv. 4 5, 12, 17, 29–33, 40. Our Lord had directed that prophets were to be known by their moral fruits (St. Matt vii. 15, 16). St. John also directs that utterances claiming inspiration should be tested by the rule of faith (1 John iv. 1–3., 2 John 7–11; cf. 1 Thess. v. 19, 21).... So St. Peter exercises prophetic power (Acts v. 3–10) and the Spirit guides the Apostles on critical occasions by specially communicated directions or prohibitions (Acts x. 19, xiii. 2, xvi. 6, xx. 22, 23). St. Paul (1 Tim. i. 18, iv. 14) says that Timothy was pointed out for his office by prophecies, and that prophecy was the means by which he came to receive his "gift". It is also the prophetic function to exhort and confirm and edify.[31]

The Christian prophet spoke not in a state of ecstasy or *amentia*, but retaining his consciousness and self-control (1 Cor 14:29–33).[32] "This state was one of intense thought, in which the attention was fastened upon a text or passage, and its application to recent events."[33] Prophets spoke at the direction of the Holy Spirit—edifying, instructing, and encouraging by means of their supernatural understanding and application of Scripture (1 Cor 14:3).

Although the word *prophet* brings to our minds someone who sees future events, foretelling was not a prophet's primary function in the ecclesiae—though it was clearly included on occasion (Agabus in Acts 11:28 and 21:11). "The Prophets' function first of all," says Selwyn, "was to search the Scriptures in order to find types of the Messiah and His kingdom, and to apply them to current events as their fulfilments, and then to declare the application."[34]

When the prophets cited the Old Testament Scriptures, they relied on the Septuagint translation almost exclusively, despite its glaring inac-

---

31. Gore, *Church and Ministry*, 353–56.
32. Lindsay, 94.
33. Selwyn, *St. Luke the Prophet*, 36.
34. Ibid., 21.

curacies.[35] But the prophets cited many other writings too—both deuterocanonical (the Apocrypha) and uncanonical Scriptures. Their use of Scripture fell into four classes: (1) prophetic, (2) authoritative, (3) historical, and (4) literary.[36] W. E. Ball provides numerous examples of each, but it would take us too far afield to reproduce them here.[37]

The use of deuterocanonical and uncanonical Scripture by the prophets and New Testament authors implies a certain respect for those writings that is not shared today. Ball points out that "though the method of citation [of uncanonical Scripture] does not perhaps necessarily imply a belief that the works cited were inspired, there is at any rate a strong presumption that this belief was entertained."[38] Origen (c. 185–254 CE) was aware of the use of uncanonical Scripture by the New Testament authors. "Many passages are cited by the Apostles and Evangelists and inserted in the New Testament which we nowhere read in those Scriptures which we call canonical, but which are nevertheless found in uncanonical books or are taken from them."[39]

The Christian prophets were especially fond of the uncanonical book *Enoch*, as Selwyn describes:

> [*Enoch*] was eminently prophetic both in its origin and in its preservation. Hardly the Book of Daniel itself was more treasured by the Prophets, partly because this remarkable book struck out a new line. A Hellenist writer quoted by Eusebius says that Enoch was the founder of what we should call astronomy. The Assumption of Moses (about A.D.) probably and the Book of Jubilees (before 70 A.D.) certainly used Enoch. The Apocalypse of Baruch (soon after 70 A.D.) depends upon it. Fourth Ezra (81–96 A.D.?) uses it often. The Testaments of the [Twelve] Patriarchs refer to it often. The Epistle of Barnabas (70–132 A.D.) cites it three times, twice as Scripture. Justin Martyr and Irenaeus use it. Athenagoras (170 A.D.) regards Enoch as a true Prophet. Tertullian (197–223 A.D.) regards Enoch as "Scripture" and "a most ancient Prophet". Clement of Alexandria (200 A.D.) quotes him by name twice as an authority.[40]

---

35. Ball, 144–47.

36. Ibid. 135.

37. Ball, 134–218. Chapters 9–12 of his work provide a full treatment of these four uses of three types of Scripture.

38. Ball, 212.

39. Ibid., 159.

40. Selwyn, *The Christian Prophets*, 68.

Ball adds:

> There are many proofs that [*Enoch*] was familiar to the early Church. It is quoted as authentic in the uncanonical Epistle of Barnabas (*circ.* 119 A.D.) on the one hand, and in the Cabbalistic Zohar on the other (*circ.* 180 A.D.). It is censured, along with some other uncanonical books, in the *Apostolic Constitutions*. It is cited as authoritative by . . . Irenaeus (202 A.D.), and by Clement of Alexandria (220 A.D.). . . . Whilst Origen (254 A.D.), in controversy with Celsus, denies that it possesses the authority of Holy Scripture, though he admits in other parts of his works that it is received as such by some.[41]

Referring to the citations from *Enoch* in 2 Pet 2:4 and Jude 6, Ball notes: "For these statements there is no authority in Old Testament Scripture, yet they are made not as though some new and original matter were unfolded, but incidentally, as in reference to things well known to the reader, and therefore apt to enforce the argument, which is the same in each case, namely, that judgment will surely overtake the wicked."[42]

Not only were the Christian prophets fond of uncanonical books like *Enoch*, but they used the canonical Scripture in ways that contradict current principles of sound hermeneutics. For the prophets in the ecclesia, Old Testament prophecy had its primary fulfillment and application to the immediate circumstances at the time it was uttered and its secondary fulfillment and application to the circumstances of some later time.[43] Selwyn adds that those things the angels desire to look into (1 Pet 1:12) are the "larger or secondary applications by Christian Prophets of [Old Testament] prophecy."[44]

What is most astounding is their disregard for the original historical circumstances or context of Scripture. Instead, the Christian prophets were focused on the *sensus plenior*.[45] Context seems to have played little to no role, as Selwyn demonstrates:[46] the prophets often took various

---

41. Ball, 160–61. For the unusual events surrounding the rediscovery of the *Enoch* manuscript, 161–70.

42. Ball, 164.

43. Selwyn, *St. Luke the Prophet*, 124.

44. Ibid., 126.

45. The deeper meaning intended by God, but not necessarily known by the human author.

46. Selwyn, *St. Luke the Prophet*, 133; *The Christian Prophets*, 62–64. For those inter-

and uncorrelated pieces of Old Testament passages (sometimes three or more) and strung them together to form an entirely new thought—all completely out of context. This same prophetic method appears in the letters of Paul and Peter, the books of Revelation and Hebrews, as well as the "fulfillment passages" in the synoptic Gospels.[47]

The Christian prophets continually searched for the will of God in the Old Testament Scriptures, as it was shown to them, and where they were to find its fulfillment. Those without the gift were cautioned against private interpretation of the Old Testament. From the prophet's viewpoint, private interpretation was impossible, since interpretation was "limited to Christian Prophets endowed with the Holy Spirit ... hence false prophets are a snare and a danger, and will be punished."[48] First Peter states that revelation was made to the prophets because they were the ones entrusted with the use and application of its contents and bound to pass them on. Any expropriation of these prophetic powers was unlawful.[49]

---

ested, I give a brief excerpt from Selwyn's full example: "elements could be recombined, and the language in which they were couched was at the disposal of the living voice. . . . [Rev] vi. 10 = Zech i. 12 'How long, O Lord, wilt thou not' (shew mercy) + Deut xxxii. 43 'avenge the blood of (his sons)' + Hosea iv. 1 'judge them that dwell on the earth'. . . " For Selwyn's complete example, see *The Christian Prophets*, 62–64.

47. "Thus in Matthew ii. 15 it is said that the child Jesus was taken into Egypt, and remained there until the death of Herod. 'That it might be fulfilled which was spoken of the Lord by the prophet, saying, Out of Egypt have I called My Son.' The reference can only be to Hosea xi. 1 'When Israel was a child, then I loved him, and called My Son out of Egypt.' In this case it is difficult to regard the words of Hosea as conveying a prediction of an incident in the career of the Messiah. Still there are theologians who contend that the prophet was consciously using the childhood of the Jewish people as an allegory or type of the childhood of our Lord. According to another view, the type or allegory existed, not in the mind of the prophet but in that of the Evangelist; and in support of this view it is pointed out that the Hebrew Targumists were fond of drawing similar analogies, and introducing them in similar language, as constituting the 'fulfilment' of prophecy. These so-called 'typical prophecies' may perhaps be more properly regarded as 'literary allusions', and so falling under the fourth of the classes I have indicated." Ball, 136–37.

48. Selwyn, *St. Luke the Prophet*, 129.

49. "In 2 Peter 1 the readers, who are not in the first instance the same as those of 1 Peter, are warned that private interpretation of the O.T. proves to be impossible, that the interpretation is limited to Christian Prophets endowed with the Holy Spirit, that the Prophets of old themselves only spake when moved by the Spirit; hence false prophets are a snare and a danger, and will be punished. Next: in 1 Peter we are told of a Messiah-spirit animating and possessing the Christian prophets as it possessed the O.T. prophets. In 2 Peter we are told of a Holy Spirit which bore or carried them. There is no difference here but one of form and metaphor. Lastly, we learn from 1 Peter that the revelation was made to Prophets because they were the body entrusted with the ministration of its contents

Barnabas, Simeon, Lucius, Manaen, Saul, Judas, and Silas (Acts 13:1; 15:32) were prophets (and teachers, since these two gifts are often intertwined). Agabus resembled the Old Testament prophets by his use of visual elements (Acts 11:28). Philip the evangelist had four prophet daughters (Acts 21:9).[50] All prophets encouraged, taught, and edified the assemblies (Acts 15:32), and, when present at meetings, the local ministry voluntarily deferred to them. The circuit or wandering apostles and prophets moved from place to place at the direction of the Holy Spirit, establishing congregations, teaching, and exhorting believers.

Yet, not every prophet was trustworthy. "Christianity attracted men then as now; they were curious about it; they seized on sides of the new religion which they could best appreciate, and could so present their beliefs as to be able to plead that they themselves were Christians of a more sympathetic character and with a wider outlook than others."[51] Jesus had warned of false prophets (Matt 7:15–20; 24:11, 24; Mark 13:22). Peter warned of false prophets (2 Pet 2:1). Hence, discernment (*diakrisis*) was crucial. Paul expected his congregations to use the gift of discernment—the supernatural power to discern truth from error—to judge even his own instructions to them (1 Cor 14:37; 1 Thess 5:20–21). John encouraged discernment as well (1 John 4:1–3). Without the exercise of this gift of discernment, the ecclesia could drift into error and heresy.[52] Hence, congregations were admonished to test the "spirit of the prophets" to determine if it was the voice of the Shepherd (John 10:5).

> The question was: Were the contents of the prophetic message such as would come from the spirit of Jesus? had it the self-evidencing ring about it? had it the true ethical meaning which must be in a message from the Master? —something which distinguished it

---

and bound in duty to pass them on as the gospel, by means of the preachers who announced them to the readers. And from 2 Peter we learn that no usurpation of prophetic powers is lawful, though the prophets now, as of old, are human beings, and the last word 'men' is not without its emphasis." Selwyn, *St. Luke the Prophet*, 129–30.

50. It is doubtful that women prophets assumed the same roles as male prophets in the ecclesia, given the limitations placed on teaching and leading in both Jewish and Gentile congregations. But, women did serve as deacons (Rom 16:1), so it may have been permitted in some context unknown to us.

51. Lindsay, 101.

52. Ibid., 100.

from everything heathenish or Jewish, something which showed that the prophet had drunk deeply at the well of Christ?[53]

Discernment was a necessary complement to the prophetic gift, and it was presumed to be active in each congregation.[54] Any authority surrendered to the prophets, any deference shown to them, was solely at the discretion of the congregation.[55] The *Didache* describes how the congregations tested the prophets, and we will examine it shortly. But discernment was *never* delegated by the congregation to any single individual or to any select group of spiritual leaders. No scriptural support exists for the gift of discernment held by proxy or in custodianship.

Although H. J. Wotherspoon acknowledges that Christian prophets were present in the ecclesia, he denies they were extraordinary.[56] He also denies that evidence exists for a twofold ministry, as Lindsay and others assert—oddly, even while admitting Scripture supports the idea.[57] He says, "A prophet's business is to prophesy, not to command. . . . There is nothing at all to suggest that prophets governed or dominated, or that they peregrinated with a function of oversight, or that local Churches depended upon them for special ministries or services."[58] But Wotherspoon

---

53. Ibid., 102.
54. Ibid., 102.
55. Ibid., 99–100.
56. Wotherspoon, 203–204.
57. "It is upon these passages [1 Cor 12:28; Eph 2:20, 3:5, 4:11] that the theory of Twofold Ministry really obtains a claim to consideration, for which otherwise there would be comparatively slight ground. They undoubtedly serve to show that in Paul's mind prophecy was a fact of vast significance, and that the prophet—the person, that is, through whom in practice prophecy exercised its function in the Church—was a person essential to the development of the Divine purpose in Christ Jesus." Wotherspoon, 149–50.
58. Wotherspoon, 145–46. Wotherspoon notes the double function of the apostle: pastoral care of the ecclesiae and evangelization. He also speaks of subordinates and delegates. "But in all this, it is with a working staff, a practical organisation, that we have to do, and not with a charismatic ministry—with apostolic agencies which are not self-validated and are not qualified only by gift and are not irresponsible, but are selected and are sent and are accountable to the authority which they represent." Wotherspoon, 132. Wotherspoon asks: "What, then, is the prophet? He is the man to whom the mind of God is revealed. . . . In both Old Testament and New, trance and vision appear as modes of prophecy, but must be accounted as lower forms of it and among those which may 'fail' and cease: as the higher and essential prophecy cannot. Trance and vision may occur to persons who are not prophets; Ananias was no more than 'a certain disciple'; and it is improbable that Pilate's wife was a prophetess. If apocalypse is also to be reckoned with

both misrepresents the nature of the twofold ministry and simultaneously imposes an incorrect definition of apostles and prophets. What he fails to understand is that the congregation and local ministry deferred to the prophets *voluntarily*, and *only after* congregational judgment of their message.[59] There was no despotism by the prophets, as Wotherspoon suggests.

Wotherspoon says, "If the *Didache* [referring to *Did.* 15.1] tells us anything on that subject, it is that local communities are not upon [the prophetic ministry's] scheme thus dependent, since bishops and deacons also minister the ministry of prophets and teachers, whatever that is understood to have been."[60] But Wotherspoon sees a conflict where none exists.[61] Not all prophets were on circuit. Furthermore, the local ministry and the prophetic ministry were not mutually exclusive.[62]

We will examine later how and why the prophetic ministry—the adhesive that bound together the various congregations—was eclipsed in the second century. Eventually, it was removed completely from its historic position of authority and replaced, first, by a single man—the pastor or bishop—and, subsequently, by an established clergy with the bishop at its head.

THE LOCAL MINISTRY

The local ministry consisted of pastors, teachers, elders, and deacons. No single man was at the head of the ecclesia, and none ever received a salary.[63] Members of the local ministry were democratically chosen by the entire congregation. Their formal task was to ensure that each member was encouraged and not in material or spiritual need. Lindsay states that

---

prophecy, it would seem to be rather a 'by-product' of its energy—St. Paul clearly differentiates it from prophecy, grouping it with a class of utterances whose common characteristic is that they interpret or have need of interpretation—while prophecy rather calls for the exercise of discrimination (1 Cor. xiv. 26–29)." Wotherspoon, 133–34.

59. Lindsay, 99.

60. Wotherspoon, 68.

61. Selwyn comments on this tendency in academic circles: "The power which some people possess of seeing difficulties where there are none is far greater than any man's power of solving true difficulties." Selwyn, *St. Luke the Prophet*, 127.

62. Lindsay, 66; Selwyn, *Luke the Prophet*, 202 n. 1, 248.

63. Beaty's work, *Paying the Pastor*, provides a complete scriptural and historical examination of this subject.

"later writings, both within and without the New Testament Canon, make it plain that these services were rendered by two classes of officials who bore official names which still exist within the Christian Church . . . pastors, overseers, elders, and deacons."[64] Yet, as Eberhard Arnold writes, "in those first years, terms for leaders like 'overseers,' 'presidents,' or 'elders,' were not clearly defined."[65]

One thing is certain, however: where mentioned, the local ministry was always *collegiate*—at least in the early years.[66] Hatch notes: "With the exception—which is probably rather apparent than real—of two passages in the Pastoral Epistles, all general references to Church officers in Apostolic and subapostolic literature speak of them in the plural."[67] It is also significant that, when Paul writes to an ecclesia, he never writes to the elders, but to the congregation as a whole.[68]

EARLY MEETINGS

Generally, each ecclesia held three distinct meetings: (1) the meeting for edification by prayer and exhortation, (2) the meeting for thanksgiving, which began with a common meal and ended with the Lord's Supper, and (3) the meeting for the business affairs of the congregation.[69]

The meeting for edification—"meeting for the Word"—was a gathering of believers for exhortation, congregational singing, prayer, and the reading aloud from the Old Testament (commonly, the Septuagint), deuterocanonical and uncanonical writings, and the "memoirs of the Apostles,"[70] as Justin Martyr (c. 100–165 CE) calls them—by which he means the Gospels. Reading Scripture aloud was the most common transmission of the teachings of Jesus and the doctrines of the faith. All Jews were literate,[71] but the same could not be said for the other races in the empire. And we know that Paul expected his letters to the congregations would be read aloud and even shared with neighboring congregations.

---

64. Lindsay, 152.
65. Arnold, *The Early Christians*, 31–32.
66. Lindsay, 152.
67. Hatch, 83.
68. Lindsay, 58–59.
69. Lindsay, 43–44.
70. Justin *1 Apol.* 67, ed. Roberts and Donaldson, 1:186.
71. Edersheim, 1:231–33. Greek was the predominant language in the empire.

The subapostolic writings indicate this was the common practice of all congregations throughout the empire, and it played a significant role in the formation of the New Testament canon.

Each member of the ecclesia was encouraged to participate in the meeting for the Word, as Paul describes it (1 Cor 14:26). Members could contribute a hymn, some memorized portion of the Scriptures, or a testimony of faith for the benefit or exhortation of all. If a prophet were present—and *only* with the approval of the congregation—he would lead the meeting and also present whatever message he had been given by the Holy Spirit. At the conclusion of his message, not simply those with the gift of discernment, but all were expected to judge whether the prophet's message was to be accepted or rejected. We noted earlier that, while these prophets were highly esteemed, they were also carefully judged, as Paul notes (1 Cor 14:29). The *Didache* describes this process.

The *Didache*, or the *Teaching of the Twelve*—a document once considered lost—was rediscovered in 1873. It is an anonymous, early Christian manual read by many congregations in the years before the New Testament was codified. Its date of composition is estimated to be from 70 to 100 CE. Since its rediscovery, it has been a vexation to those who insist on an ordained clergy. Consequently, many have attempted to minimize its significance.

Wotherspoon disputes its relevance, value, and provenance.[72] But, as Selwyn notes,

> There is no reason why we should consider, as some writers maintain, that the [*Didache*] represents a curious and abnormal set of rules, accepted only by some outlying district in Egypt or elsewhere. So far from thrusting this valuable relic back into a corner, we ought to welcome it as a witness to what was the accepted code of the main current of the Christian Church for the greater part of the period 40–75 A.D.[73]

Philip Schaff considers it valuable and believes it adds significantly to our understanding of early Christian worship and doctrine. That the *Didache* is doctrinally meager, Philip Schaff says, proves nothing.[74]

---

72. Wotherspoon, 50–75.
73. Selwyn, *St. Luke the Prophet*, 28.
74. Schaff, *Teaching of the Twelve*, 22–23.

He counts it older than *Barnabas*,⁷⁵ says that it is remarkably similar in tone and substance to James,⁷⁶ and that it clearly supports the twofold ministry.⁷⁷

The *Didache* describes how the gift of discernment operated in the early congregations. Any prophet who failed the test was immediately rejected.

> Whosoever then comes and teaches you all the things aforesaid, receive him. But if the teacher himself being perverted teaches another teaching to the destruction [of this], hear him not, but if [he teach] to the increase of righteousness and the knowledge of the Lord, receive him as the Lord. Now with regard to the Apostles and Prophets, according to the decree (command) of the gospel, so do ye. Let every Apostle that cometh to you be received as the Lord. But he shall not remain [longer than] one day; and, if need be, another [day] also; but if he remain three [days] he is a false prophet. And when the Apostle departeth, let him take nothing except bread [enough] till he reach his lodging (night-quarters). But if he ask for money, he is a false prophet. And every prophet who speaks in the spirit ye shall not try or prove; for every sin shall be forgiven, but this sin shall not be forgiven. Not every one that speaks in the spirit is a Prophet, but only if he has the behavior (the ways) of the Lord. By their behavior then shall the false prophet and the [true] Prophet be known. And no Prophet that orders a table in the spirit eats of it [himself], unless he is a false prophet. And every Prophet who teaches the truth if he does not practice what he teaches, is a false prophet. . . . But whosoever says in the spirit: Give me money or any other thing, ye shall not listen to him; but if he bid you to give for others that lack, let no one judge him.⁷⁸

The *Didache* shows that the apostles and prophets were highly esteemed and honored in the congregations, but that they were accepted only after passing judgment by the ecclesia—judgment of both their message and actions, or fruit. By means of this essential and necessary discernment, the local ecclesia maintained its true discipleship. To neglect this responsibility was to court spiritual shipwreck and judgment (Rev 2:1–3:22).

---

75. Ibid., 19–20.
76. Ibid., 26.
77. Ibid., 66.
78. *Did.* 11:1–10, 12, ed. Schaff, *Teaching of the Twelve*, 198–204.

The second meeting—the meeting for fellowship or thanksgiving—was a communal meal, known as the Agape. As noted earlier, it was similar to the common meals of Roman confraternities. J. F. Keating points out that Jesus "repeatedly spoke of his Kingdom under the image of a Supper. . . . And this symbolism naturally survived and developed in the infant Christian community in the shape of common meals."[79] Each member of the Christian congregation contributed to this feast, by supplying something he or she had purchased at the market[80] or prepared at home, as each was able. The Agape was both a social and religious gathering, but was closed to those outside the ecclesia. It was convivial and similar to a covered-dish supper, where members of the community considered themselves guests at Messiah's table.[81] Their behavior was expected to be appropriate to that idea—although, we know Paul had to correct and remind the ecclesia at Corinth about the solemnity of the feast and the danger of treating it otherwise (1 Cor 11:23–34).

The highlight of the Agape was the celebration of the "Lord's Supper,"[82] which was observed at the conclusion of the meal. If a prophet was present, he would offer prayer and thanksgiving before the memorial. After a final prayer and hymn, any food left over was distributed to the needy—first to the poor members of the congregation and then any outside the ecclesia. These remaining "first fruits" were never distributed to the pastors, elders, or deacons, unless they were also part of the groups that normally received support—prophets, widows, orphans, and the poor.[83] Like all other members of the ecclesia, the local ministry was expected to earn a living and contribute to the Agape.

The Agape did not survive the second century. It was eventually truncated to the Lord's Supper, for reasons we will examine later. Until the close of the first century, Christians considered both the Agape and

---

79. Keating, 160.

80. Most Romans and provincials preferred a predominantly vegetarian diet. Meat was not a staple, as it is today, even for the wealthy (Fowler, 32–40). Some meat sold in shops or on the street had been obtained from a pagan temple or priest before being sold. One might also partake of a communal meal in some temples or their adjacent grounds and parks. See MacMullen, 36–40. This is the background of Paul's discussion of meat sacrificed to idols (1 Cor 8:1–13; 10:19–33).

81. Pagans also expected the presence of their god at communal banquets. See MacMullen, 38–40.

82. It was later designated the Eucharist, or "blessing."

83. *Did.* 13; Lindsay, 202.

baptism sacred events, in that Jesus walked amongst them during their observance. But this sacred aspect was devoid of the superstition and trappings that later attached to them, embellishing and converting them into institutional rites dispensed by a select caste.

The third meeting of the ecclesia was for the financial and business affairs of the congregation. Since each ecclesia was a democracy, the financial matters pertaining to the community were discussed openly by the entire congregation—women as well as men. At this meeting, letters of commendation were drawn up, deputies or messengers were selected and dispatched, and any conflicts among believers were discussed and adjudicated.[84]

At this meeting, the congregation "expelled unworthy members . . . deliberated upon and came to conclusions about the restoration of brethren who had fallen away and showed signs of repentance . . . arrived at its decisions when necessary by voting, and the vote of the majority decided the case."[85] The meeting for business also provided an opportunity for each member to contribute as he was able and willing—either in commodities or funds—for the general distribution to those of the ecclesia who were in need, or others who were not believers, as the congregation determined. As with "the Seven," these gifts were distributed by those chosen from the ecclesia for that task, and we see this practice encouraged in Paul's writings (1 Cor 16:3). We know that those in need within the community were the primary, and almost exclusive, recipients. But the ecclesia shared its common store with outsiders, whenever possible. This was the way the confraternities of the empire operated in the secular world, and the ecclesiae adopted the practice.

The congregation expected the presence of the Lord Jesus at each meeting, and members conducted themselves accordingly. The ecclesia presumed that the Lord would supply all necessary spiritual gifts that made them a complete body. Although his list is not exhaustive, Paul enumerates the spiritual gifts present in the ecclesia (1 Cor 12:4–11). But of all the gifts, none was more valuable and cherished than the gift of prophecy and its counterpart, the gift of discernment.

No single pastor or elder was ever responsible for edification or teaching in the early years. Each ecclesia had its collegiate, local ministry

---

84. Lindsay., 54–55.

85. Ibid., 55.

comprised of pastors, elders, and deacons—all plural. None received a salary. These democratically elected men were subservient to the apostles and prophets, who always led the meetings, when present and permitted to do so by the congregation. Above all else, each ecclesia was independent in the Lord and ran its own affairs.

> The evidence for the independence and self-government of the churches to which St. Paul addressed his epistles is so overwhelming that it is impossible even to imagine the presence within them of any ecclesiastical authority with an origin and power independent of the assembly of the congregation, and the apostle does not make the slightest allusion to any such governing or controlling authority, whether vested in one man or in a group of men.[86]

These early forms of leadership, organization, and meetings survived until nearly the last decade of the first century. By that time, the original apostles and prophets had all been removed from history. As we will see shortly, confusion and temptations, resulting from various heresies and persecutions, strained this simple organizational model. In an effort to combat what the local ministry perceived as a danger, some ecclesiae began to formulate new theories that would hold the congregations together amidst the storm and establish a united front—even if it meant introducing alien ideas and internal structures.

---

86. Ibid., 58.

3

Early Christian Life

"We are apt to forget," remarks Lindsay, "that Christianity came to establish a new social living as well as a religion, and that from the first it demanded that all relations between man and man ought to be regulated by Christian principles."[1] The new demands Lindsay speaks of were not restricted to fellow Christians, but included interaction with nonbelievers as well. Christians are distinct from those around them, who do not have faith in Messiah, but that distinction is by grace—it does not make us more intrinsically valuable or important than those who do not have faith. But it produces conflict with the world and, in that conflict, we are neither to be conformed by the world nor attempt to conform the world to our standards. We are to be in the world, but not of the world.

Eberhard Arnold states in *Innerland*[2] that it is wrong to view Christian life as simply a list of rules to be followed. Such an approach is doomed to failure, since we cannot change the inner, spiritual life from the outside. Jesus explicitly stated that his new life begins at the heart of a man and works its way outward—like leaven working through dough. Being born spiritually is an almost imperceptible event, yet, over time, the Holy Spirit fills and transforms all aspects of the believer's life—if it is permitted to do so. It is the inner Word, the living Word of the Holy Spirit, that speaks to us and transforms us.

Scripture teaches that humans are in a state of separation from God, as a consequence of sin, and that no act on our part can correct this state. The law of Moses describes the demands of perfection and simultaneously exposes how sinful we are. Paul says when we attempt to abide by

---

1. Lindsay, 57.
2. Arnold, "The Inner Life" in *Innerland*, 13–38.

the law, it has a curious effect of bringing sinful urges to the surface and causing us to sin (Rom 7:9–12). The only means of escape from this hopeless situation is to acknowledge that it is impossible to achieve perfection on our own, through the law or any other action on our part. Since Jesus achieved the perfection the law demands and paid the price of death for those who cannot ever achieve it, we ask God to use his death in our stead. The moment we acknowledge we cannot do it ourselves and that Jesus achieved it for us, the new life in the Holy Spirit begins. From that moment, the Holy Spirit dwells in us, works within us—like leaven—to regenerate us from the inside. This is salvation and the new life in Messiah, and it was preached to the Jew first.

Most early converts to Christianity were Jews, as Selwyn reminds us:

> But there is no proof whatever that even so much as hundreds of Gentiles were Christians without having first become Jews. When St Paul preached to pure Gentiles, at Athens, all that we know is that his preaching produced hardly any conversions. It must always be difficult for the modern reader to place himself in thought in this interim of Christian faith between 35 and 70 AD. But he must not assume that there were very many Gentile believers before 70, and for some years after.[3]

Selwyn continues:

> We must recognise the fact that any disturbance of the old Jewish lines of belief and conduct, especially when they were changed for the purpose of admitting the heathen proselytes to the Church, and when the "door of faith" was opened alongside of the most venerable door of circumcision, must inevitably result in perversion of the true teaching, and in a disposition to torture it in order to allow loose conduct to combine with a profession of the faith.[4]

Hence, those Jews who believed in Jesus as Messiah were skeptical and suspicious of Gentile converts. In the first century, the Jews were, in many ways, more prepared than the Gentiles for this new life. Jews had separated themselves from the surrounding pagan societies for generations—admittedly, with only moderate results. Yet, there was still less

---

3. Selwyn, *St. Luke the Prophet*, 77.
4. Ibid., 260.

need to caution a Jew about sexual impurity, pagan entertainments, and contamination by idols. Jews who believed the gospel were particularly suspicious of the ability of Gentile believers to manage these areas of life, and this explains why Paul was bedeviled by those who construed his gospel as an abandonment of Judaism. In order to preclude any perversion of messianic Judaism by the Gentiles, the Judiaizers wanted to make all Gentiles Jews *first*. That attempt ultimately failed, but the turmoil resulted in the concordat of the Jerusalem council. What is surprising is that the council chose a moderate solution and agreed not to require Gentiles to become Jews. Instead, it specified minimum conduct that would protect the conscience of the messianic Jews.[5] However, for Jew and Gentile, the gospel was the same and specific conduct was expected of both.

Although many see a conflict between Paul's "justification by faith" and James's "faith without works is dead,"[6] this false dichotomy is easily removed when we look at Paul's complete presentation of the gospel. Rabbinism taught that righteousness comes through the study and practice of the Law. After his conversion, Paul understood that the Law was not an accurate representation of righteousness. Had it been so, he would have recognized Jesus as Messiah. That he didn't, and had to be struck down on the road to Damascus, was a lesson he never forgot, and it altered his view of the Mosaic law completely.[7]

Yet Paul, like James, teaches that behavior changes as a consequence of salvation, and this is clearly documented by Luke (Acts 24:25; 26:20). Paul teaches that repentance will manifest itself in action. He generalizes this concept by using the terms *goodness* and *self-control*—both are the normal outgrowth of the new life in the Spirit. Paul is not in conflict with James, for both teach that faith must express itself in action. But, for Paul, this was not a new law.

Jesus did not bring a new law. The Sermon on the Mount does not replace the Mosaic law—neither is it a new set of "rules to live by." What Jesus describes (Matt 5:1—7:28) is the natural overflow of regeneration by

---

5. Hort, 92–94. Hort notes that silence on the letter from Jerusalem after Paul's second missionary journey, when he is visiting previously established ecclesiae, is significant. Paul may have decided to inculcate the four elements of the letter by different means, or may even have doubted their expediency. Many today continue to insist on their application.

6. Luther certainly did, calling James a "letter of straw."

7. Weizsacker, 1:92–93.

the Holy Spirit. Hence, we are not to worry, but rather trust that there are no accidents in life, that our life is held closely by our Heavenly Father. We are not to resist evil, or retaliate against evil done to us, or participate in any form of wrath or retribution, because *we* have been pardoned and spared from wrath ourselves. We are not to hoard wealth or material possessions, but rather share with those who do not have them, because our home is the kingdom of God. We are to be generous to those within and outside the community. We are to forgive our enemies and those who wrong or cheat us—with a stern warning (often conveniently forgotten) that we will not be forgiven if we do not forgive.

Paul specifies further that believers are not to seek retribution through legal action in court, even if cheated (1 Cor 6:1–8).[8] We are to be thankful in all circumstances, honest in our dealings with men, and keep our speech clean and spiced with the gospel. We are not to have any sexual relationships outside the marriage bond.[9] Believers are to earn a living, so as not to be a burden and have something to share. We are to remove all bitterness, anger, and revenge from our lives. We are not to get drunk, use unseemly or filthy language, or share vulgar humor, and so on (1 Cor 6:9–10; Eph 4:25–29; 5:3–7; 5:18–20; Col 3:5–9; 1 Thess 5:13–18).

Significantly, Paul reminds us to *remember from what we have been saved* (1 Cor 6:20), and permit our bodies to be a living sacrifice to our new master, Jesus the Messiah. We are to say "no" to ourselves and understand that our relationship with this world is now that of a sojourner, an alien resident—our citizenship is in the kingdom of God. This is not a new law of Moses that attempts to achieve perfection from the outside. Instead, it is a description of the overflow from the heart after recognition of our salvation.

That Paul must continually remind his congregations shows the new life is "not reached in a single stride,"[10] but is a process of growth. Still, he clearly indicates that the absence of any fruit of the Spirit strongly suggests, at the very least, a *complete misunderstanding of salvation* (1 Cor 6:20; Eph 4:17–24). Those who claim to belong to the body of Messiah,

---

8. Dobschutz, *Christian Life in the Primitive Church*, 29–30, 57; Hatch, 73.

9. Unpalatable as it is in our time, homosexuality was labeled a sexual sin by the early ecclesia. Paul is quite clear, and uses both terms for homosexuals: ἀρσενοκοίτης (1 Cor 6:9; 1 Tim 1:10) and μαλακός (1 Cor 6:9). Those who had forsaken that behavior were accepted in the ecclesia (1 Cor 6:11).

10. Dobschutz, *Christian Life in the Primitive Church*, 10.

yet refuse to allow the Holy Spirit to gain control of their lives, must be "put out of the ecclesia,"[11] since they have deliberately cut themselves off from life in the Spirit (1 Cor 5:10–13).

Even though most Christians today are aware of these attributes of life in the Spirit, our problem is that we read them within the context of our modern, Western culture, and they have either lost their original meaning, or else have been redefined to accommodate the surrounding society. We have committed illegitimate transfer of meaning on the conduct described in the New Testament. But we can gain fresh perspective and insight by examining how the early believers understood what the New Testament describes.

When we examine how the early believers put their faith into practice, the contrast to Western Christianity today is dramatic. For the early Christians, salvation radically altered the focus of their lives and forced a separation from the surrounding pagan society. First- and second-century philosophers, satirists, and historians, like Celsus, Lucian, and Tacitus, ridiculed Christian conduct for its stark opposition to the surrounding society. Sometimes their attacks were based on ignorant speculation and rumor. But often their descriptions were acknowledged by the Christians themselves.

The sensitivities of those early believers would be just as unsettling to us as they were to their own pagan neighbors. That fact alone underscores that our Western Christian culture is more similar to the pagan Roman culture than we might expect, and it also indicates how Christian life has eroded over the centuries. As we shall see, the cause of this erosion is that the institutional church has permitted syncretism to take root through the introduction of worldly philosophies and notions. The church has perverted or ignored most of the original doctrines and the way of life that forced early Christians to separate from pagan society. We accept without a blush today what early believers would have fled from in horror.

Historically, those most receptive to the gospel have been the disenfranchised. In the first century, many converts came from the lower classes—the dregs of society—slaves, prostitutes, street urchins, criminals.[12]

---

11. The expression used in 3 John 10 is "put out" or "toss out of the church." Excommunication is a later, formalized ritual of "putting out" of the community.

12. The *Satyricon* by Gaius Petronius, friend to Nero, offers an important glimpse of the debauchery and street life of the lower classes, as well as the ostentation of the

Their low social status provided ammunition for ridicule by their critics. The second century philosopher, Celsus, described Christians converts this way:

> If there be any ignorant, or unintelligent, or uninstructed, or foolish persons, let them come with confidence. By which words, acknowledging that such individuals are worthy of their God, they manifestly show that they desire and are able to gain over only the silly, and the mean, and the stupid, with women and children.[13]

This is a typical portrait and it reflects how the educated Roman viewed Christianity.

As the gospel spread over the empire, it drew a few individuals from the upper classes, but they were generally in the minority, at least until the middle of the second century. Carl von Weizsacker notes:

> Rich people, strictly called, were hardly to be found among the followers of Jesus. His own words about the difficulty in the way of a rich man's entrance into the kingdom of heaven are decisive. Yet there were not wanting well-to-do persons who contributed to the support of Jesus and His disciples. And on the whole it cannot be said that His companions consisted exclusively of poor men. Some of them at least owed their poverty to the fact that they had left their former position and abandoned their property in order to devote themselves wholly to the cause of the Master.[14]

Most meetings of the early ecclesia were usually held in homes—if available, the home of one of the wealthier members of the congregation, since these would have a room large enough to accommodate a large congregation. We see this early in Acts, where the disciples met at the home of Mary, the mother of Mark (Acts 12:12).

> Thus far it seems pretty clear that St Paul's language points to a practice by which wealthy or otherwise important persons who had become Christians, among their other services to their brother Christians, allowed the large hall or saloon often attached to (or included in) the larger sort of private houses, to be used as places of meeting, whether for worship or for other affairs of the community. Accordingly the Ecclesia in the house of this or that man, would seem to mean that particular assemblage of Christians, out

---

uneducated wealthy in first-century Rome—for those whose conscience permits.

13. Origen *Cels.* 3.44, ed. Roberts and Donaldson, 4:481–82.
14. Weizsacker, 1:54.

of the Christians of the whole city, which was accustomed to meet under his roof. The instances are these, Aquila and Priscilla at Ephesus (1 Cor. xvi.19); the same pair afterwards at Rome (Rom. xvi. 5); Nympha (or some would say Nymphas) at Colossae (Col iv.15); and Philemon also at Colossae (Philem. 2).[15]

As Hort alludes, wealthy Christians were expected to do more than simply open their homes. The ecclesia was built upon the voluntary, yet generous, sharing of worldly wealth for the sake of poorer brothers and sisters. The wealthy members of the congregation were taught that they had received wealth as a gift from God for the sake of their poorer brethren in the ecclesia. They were expected to share their material largesse and advantages because God had provided it to them for that purpose. This was merely the continuation of the practice begun in Jerusalem and described in Acts. "It is plain that in apostolic times the primary duty overshadowing all others, was that those who had this world's goods should help their poorer brethren who had need. . . . Devotion to the invisible God was supposed to manifest itself by practical love to the visible Brethren."[16] As Weizsacker notes, "The spirit of the gospel involved not merely a helpful love of our neighbour, but also the renunciation of property as a hindrance to the service of God, and a barrier in the way of righteousness in His kingdom."[17] The Jerusalem ecclesia "concerned itself with this care of the poor, and regarded it as a duty committed to it, an essential expression of its faith."[18] Just as the Jerusalem congregation was a society that "involved far-reaching mutual obligations on the part of its members, and indeed bound them together in an alliance that embraced their whole life,"[19] so all the congregations in the empire continued in that traditional teaching.

The ecclesiae shared amongst themselves as well. Paul reminds believers in Corinth to share with other congregations in need—not to their own affliction, but in equality, knowing that other congregations will also share with them when they have need (2 Cor 8:13–15). He reminds all believers to generously sow material blessings without grudging (2 Cor 9:6–

---

15. Hort, 117–18.
16. Lindsay, 115.
17. Weizsacker, 1:56.
18. Ibid., 54.
19. Ibid., 57.

8). James sternly warns against turning away from any brethren in need, stating that such neglect indicates faith without works (Jas 2:16–18).

Wealthy members in the congregations understood their position as an opportunity, not an obligation, as William Simcox notes:

> What the Church did was to maintain the poor in comfort, by the rich sacrificing their accustomed luxuries—not to make everyone dependent for necessaries on everybody else, instead of on themselves. Moreover, it is to be noticed that while St. Barnabas sold his estate, apparently in Cyprus, his aunt retained her house at Jerusalem, and *used* it, instead of parting with it, for the benefit of the community; while we are told that Ananias was under no compulsion to emulate his charity, at least in the entireness of its extent.[20]

Justin Martyr states "Those of us who are wealthy help all those who are in want (τοῖς λειπομένοις) and we always remain together (συνέσμεν)."[21] And Aristides, a Christian apologist from the early second century, says: "And he who has gives to him who has not without grudging."[22]

The idea of sharing one's wealth with the dregs of society was questionable to the educated Roman. Since life was little more than the survival of the fittest, slaves, prostitutes, the poor, and all the other offal of society had no value. They were the retched refuse. What could possibly be gained by alleviating their hardships to extend their miserable lives? To the educated Roman, Christian charity was highly suspicious and likely concealed some ulterior, nefarious motive.

Naturally, the Christian assemblies were cautious about being observed by those outside, especially as hostility toward them grew. By holding their meetings in private dwellings, Christians were protected from prying eyes. New religions and secret meetings at night had long been forbidden by law.[23] But, even though it was illegal to introduce new reli-

---

20. Simcox, 10. Simcox notes: "If we accept the generally-received translation of Acts v. 4. But I am not sure that we should not render, 'Did it not indeed remain thine own, and though sold continue as before in thine own power?' If so, the condemnation of Ananias was in part for keeping back any of the money, not only for hypocrisy in pretending to give the whole. But if the abdication of superfluous wealth was required of all converts who had it, it still stopped short of the 'vow of poverty' in the monastic sense."

21. Justin *1 Apol.* 1.67, quoted in Keating, 60.

22. Harris, 107.

23. "No one may hold meetings at night in the city." Cicero *On the Laws* 2.19, ed. Arnold, *The Early Christians*, 59.

gions into the Roman Empire,[24] these laws were generally not enforced, as William Ramsay notes:

> Now the dislike entertained for the new religion was at first founded on the disturbance it caused in the existing relations of society. Toleration of new religions as such was far greater under the Roman Empire than it has been in modern times: in the multiplicity of religions and gods that existed in the same city, a single new addition was a matter of almost perfect indifference.[25]

Ramsay overstates toleration, however. Religious conservatism dominated the society and religious innovation in the Roman Empire was considered not only painful, but bad. " 'New' was a term of disapproval. . . . 'Old' was good."[26] Whatever religious toleration existed was generally limited by geography, as A. Taylor Innes notes:

> It is well known that the policy of Rome as a conquering power towards the religions of subject peoples was one of toleration. But that meant little more than toleration of existing religions in their local seats, or, at the farthest, in the race to which such a religion properly belonged. Because the worship of Serapis or Isis was tolerated on the Nile, as a monotheistic worship was in Judaea, it by no means followed that either of them was permitted on the banks of the Tiber. Outside the region or province where the local cult ruled—and, in the case of Jews, outside the Jewish race—it was denied the rights of publicity and of proselytism, and was restricted to a passive and a private existence. These general considerations explain some of the variations in the Roman treatment of the Jewish and Christian faiths. The old Jewish religion had the paradoxical quality of being national or local on the one hand, while on the other it claimed to be exclusive truth. The union of the two qualities went far to explain that hostility to the human race which the Romans were fond of ascribing to it. A faith which attacked that of all other men, without inviting them to share in it, invited this misconstruction. But its very want of aggressiveness saved it from collisions. When Christianity appeared, a different problem had to be dealt with. Here was a faith which not only claimed to be the absolute truth, but which refused to be confined within local limits. . . . The constitutional law of Rome reserved to the State the right on the one hand to approve and licence, and on

---

24. This was the accusation against Paul, which backfired (Acts 18:13).
25. Ramsay, 12.
26. MacMullen, 3.

the other to repress and forbid while unlicensed, the expression of new religious convictions, the public existence of a new faith.[27]

As we observed earlier, many of the congregations modeled themselves on the Roman confraternities and the client-patron relationship. For a time, Christianity successfully masked itself as merely one more of those common societies—much like our beneficent associations, clubs, and labor unions. Yet, there was still a danger in this, as Keating states:

> From the very earliest times associations or guilds of a more or less religious character had, as we have seen, been common at Rome ... and had been treated under the Republic with comparative leniency, provided that their meetings were not nocturnal or clandestine, or likely to prove prejudicial to the public safety. But under the Empire much stricter watch began to be kept over them. Julius, and later Augustus, suppressed all "*collegia*" which seemed likely to prove dangerous. Only those that were venerable from their antiquity, or obviously harmless, were allowed to survive; and new foundations were prohibited if they were without special permission, which was but sparingly given. This supervision was most strictly exercised by the wisest and best of the Emperors.[28]

The greatest secret order is the kingdom of God.[29] But secrecy always entices speculation. Those outside the ecclesiae passed along lurid tales and rumors of nocturnal iniquities practiced in darkness. Minucius Felix, an apologist of the second century, records what pagans believed:

> Having gathered together from the lowest dregs the more unskilled, and women, credulous and, by the facility of their sex, yielding, establish a herd of a profane conspiracy, which is leagued together by nightly meetings, and solemn fasts, and inhuman meats—not by any sacred rite, but by that which requires expiation—a people skulking and shunning the light, silent in public, but garrulous in corners. They despise the temples as dead-houses, they reject the gods, they laugh at sacred things. . . . Oh, wondrous folly and incredible audacity! they despise present torments, although they fear those which are uncertain and future; and while they fear to die after death, they do not fear to die for the present. . . . They know one another by secret marks and insignia and they love one another almost before they know one another. Everywhere also

---

27. Innes, 114–17.
28. Keating, 96–97.
29. Robertson, 144.

there is mingled among them a certain religion of lust, and they call one another promiscuously brothers and sisters.... I hear that they adore the head of an ass.... Some say that they worship the [genitals] of their pontiff and priest, and adore the nature, as it were, of their common parent. An infant covered over with meal, that it may deceive the unwary, is placed before him who is to be stained with their rites: this infant is slain by the young pupil, who has been urged on as if to harmless blows on the surface of the meal, with dark and secret wounds.... They lick up its blood; eagerly they divide its limbs. By this victim they are pledged together; with this consciousness of wickedness they are covenanted to mutual silence.... On a solemn day they assemble at the feast, with all their children, sisters, mothers, people of every sex and of every age. There, after much feasting, when the fellowship has grown warm, and the fervour of incestuous lust has grown hot with drunkenness, a dog that has been tied to the [lamp] is provoked.... And thus the conscious light being overturned and extinguished in the shameless darkness, the connections of abominable lust involve them.... Why do they endeavour with such pains to conceal and to cloak whatever they worship, since honourable things always rejoice in publicity, while crimes are kept secret? Why have they no altars, no temples, no acknowledged images? Why do they never speak openly, never congregate freely, unless for the reason that what they adore and conceal is either worthy of punishment, or something to be ashamed of?... Because they threaten conflagration to the whole world, and to the universe itself, with all its stars, are they meditating its destruction?[30]

Christians were a scandal to the cultured and educated Roman. They either worshipped an invisible God who had no temple—therefore, were atheists—or they worshipped as God a common criminal who had been crucified in Judea—which was absurd. Celsus writes, "If [Christ] had chanced to have been cast from a precipice, or thrust into a pit, or suffocated by hanging, or had been a leather-cutter, or stone-cutter, or worker in iron, there would have been (invented) a precipice of life beyond the heavens, or a pit of resurrection, or a cord of immortality, or a blessed stone, or an iron of love, or a sacred leather!"[31]

Yet, it was not so much the novelty of their religion, their secret meetings, their strange generosity, or even the social class of their ad-

---

30. Minucius Felix *Oct.* 8–10, ed. Roberts and Donaldson, 4:177–78.
31. Origen *Cels.* 6.34.

herents, but rather their separation from and antagonism toward Roman society that attracted the most attention from both the populace and the magistrate.

> The first way in which Christianity excited the popular enmity, outside the Jewish community, was by disturbing the existing state of society and trade, and not by making innovations in religion.[32]

Indeed, the resistance to Roman society led those with a vested interest in that society to reject Christianity.

> The aggressiveness of Christianity, the change in social habits and everyday life which it introduced, and the injurious effect that it sometimes exercised on trades which were encouraged by paganism, combined with the intolerance that it showed for other religions, made it detested among people who regarded with equanimity, or even welcomed, the introduction into their cities of the gods of Greece, of Rome, of Egypt, of Syria.[33]

Most educated Romans no longer believed in the gods, or else considered them otiose. The uneducated were driven by superstition and fear. But all members of society were expected to conform to pagan social standards, at least for the sake of appearance. Decent Roman conduct demanded it. Paganism was insidious and infiltrated every waking moment.

Roman parents, like all parents, were anxious for the well-being of their children. The superstition that pervaded society added to their anxiety. "The gods were simple beneficent powers who divided amongst them the business of superintending the earthly fortunes of their Roman children," says Charles Bigg.

> For this purpose they were assisted by numerous subordinates. Thus Flora looked after the farmer's meadows, Epona after his horses, his bees were the care of Mellona, his fruit of Pomona, his lambs of Pales, the boundary-stone that marked the limits of his little estate of Terminus. Every detail of work, every moment of life, was under the charge of some divinity who had nothing else to care for. Thus the child was guarded by Iterduca and Domiduca, who led him safely through the perils of the crowded streets, while his school lessons and his budding intelligence were watched over

---

32. Ramsay, 130.
33. Ibid., 12.

by Mens, Deus Catius Pater, Consus, Sentia, Volumnus, Stimula, Peta, and others. When these had discharged their task they handed him over to Juventas and Fortuna Barbata, whose office it was to protect the adolescent. They are more like fairies than gods, these kindly limited little elves, these patrons of the nursery, the school, and the plough.[34]

The gospel was preached in the midst of an intricate and ubiquitous paganism, and the Christians were suspect by their conspicuous abandonment of and separation from these normal and polite religious and social standards. After conversion, the Christian was careful to ostracize himself from even a hint of his former pagan life.

> The public spectacles were an essential part of the cheerful devotion of the Pagans, and the gods were supposed to accept, as the most grateful offering, the games that the prince and people celebrated in honour of their peculiar festivals. The Christian, who with pious horror avoided the abomination of the circus or the theatre, found himself encompassed with infernal snares in every convivial entertainment, as often as his friends, invoking the hospitable deities, poured out libations to each other's happiness. When the bride, struggling with well-affected reluctance, was forced in hymenaeal pomp over the threshold of her new habitation, or when the sad procession of the dead slowly moved towards the funeral pile, the Christian, on these interesting occasions, was compelled to desert the persons who were the dearest to him, rather than contract the guilt inherent to those impious ceremonies. Every art and every trade that was in the least concerned in the framing or adorning of idols was polluted by a stain of idolatry; a severe sentence, since it devoted to eternal misery the far greater part of the community, which is employed in the exercise of liberal or mechanic professions.[35]

From the perspective of the Roman populace, Christians no longer participated in the everyday affairs of society that permitted men to be considered a responsible part of that society. They stopped attending the games and circus. They no longer participated in politics.[36] They

---

34. Bigg, 8.
35. Gibbon, 1:185.
36. It is a common misconception that inhabitants of the Roman Empire had no voice in government; therefore, it is claimed, Christians today, who have an opportunity, also have an obligation to vote. True, the empire was hardly democratic—in the sense of one man, one vote. And, as with most republics, Roman law favored the wealthy. But

no longer celebrated the customary feast days, or political and religious holidays. They refused the sword—indeed, any form of retribution or violence. They fled from anything associated with the coarse and worldly life around them. But it was dangerous to withdraw from these social obligations, as Bigg notes:

> On a stated day delegates from the cities assembled in the metropolls, business was transacted, and there was a great festival at which games, especially those of the arena, were celebrated. The president of these great gatherings was the High Priest of the province, and the special religious intention was the worship of the Genius of Caesar and of Rome. Once a year, therefore, when large multitudes were drawn together by local patriotism and by the desire for amusement, when the whole country-side was alive with excitement, the Christian was brought face to face with this cruel embarrassment. If he stayed away he was regarded not only as a kill-joy but as a bad citizen, if he attended how could he escape idolatry? Do what he would he could hardly avoid giving offence. If the mob caught sight of his long face, they might shout out his name. The lions were there all ready: criminals might perhaps be scarce, and Caesar's enemy had no friends. It was in this way that two of the worst massacres of the second century occurred, that of Smyrna in which Polycarp met his end, and that of Lyons.[37]

The early Christians were so distinct that Aristides called them a *genus tertium* (third race[38])—neither Greek nor Roman, neither man nor woman, neither Gentile nor Jew. And, just as Jews had been, Christians were labeled *odium generis humani* (haters of mankind) because they insisted upon living uncontaminated by the surrounding culture. Their separation and opposition to the surrounding society was so conspicuous that the populace considered Christians unfit to live. They were worse

---

Christians declined to participate in politics (meager as it was) and government because of their new status as sojourners—alien residents. For them, government was an instrument of wrath and fostered nationalism. Thus, Christians could not participate or hold office in it. These concepts were recovered by the Radical Reformers in the sixteenth century.

37. Bigg, 16–17.

38. There may be allusions to "the third race" in the Paul's letter to the Ephesians. Jesus' death and resurrection has broken down the dividing wall between these two races and has created a new race. Paul alludes to these three races: "Do not cause anyone to stumble, whether Jews, Greeks, or the Church of God" (1 Cor 10:32).

than Jews—who at least participated in the commercial and political interests of society.

This was no misconception by the Roman populace. The early believers scrupulously attempted to avoid anything they considered inappropriate to their profession of faith in Jesus and his kingdom. They saw themselves as alien residents, ambassadors[39] of the kingdom of God, heralds of peace, mercy, and pardon. And each believer inspected his daily conduct and words as they appeared to those outside the faith.

The refusal of Christians to hold political office, participate in political affairs, or join the military prompted Celsus to taunt: "if all were to do the same as you, there would be nothing to prevent his being left in utter solitude and desertion, and the affairs of the earth would fall into the hands of the wildest and most lawless barbarians." To this Origen responded:

> Celsus urges us "to help the king with all our might, and to labour with him in the maintenance of justice, to fight for him; and if he requires it, to fight under him, or lead an army along with him." . . . We do, when occasion requires, give help to kings, and that, so to say, a divine help, putting on the whole armour of God. . . . Do not those who are priests at certain shrines, and those who attend on certain gods, as you account them, keep their hands free from blood, that they may with hands unstained and free from human blood offer the appointed sacrifices to your gods. . . . You never enlist the priests in the army. . . . We do not indeed fight under [the emperor], although he require it; but we fight on his behalf, forming a special army—an army of piety—by offering our prayers to God.[40]

In order to understand how the early believers examined their daily conduct, let's briefly return to the *Didache*. That entire document hangs upon its opening statement:

> There are two ways, one of life and one of death; but there is a great difference between the two ways.[41]

---

39. When Paul states, "We are ambassadors for Christ" (2 Cor 5:20; cf. Eph 4:20), his words "stand out in quite different relief when we know that πρεσβεύω, 'I am an ambassador,' and the corresponding substantive πρεσβευτής, 'ambassador,' were the proper terms in the Greek East for the Emperor's Legate." Deissmann, 379.

40 Origen *Cels.* 8.68, 73.

41. *Did.* 1.1.

This figure of the "Two Ways" had its origin in Judaism. It is a teaching woven throughout both Old and New Testaments and clearly set forth in Deut 11:26–28; 30:1, 15–19; 1 Kgs 18:21; Jer 21:8; Matt 7:13–14; 2 Pet 2:2, 15, 21. It also appears in extracanonical works like *Barnabas*, *Shepherd*, the *Apostolic Constitutions*,[42] and in the deuterocanonical book Ecclesiasticus, where we read

> Good is set over against evil, and life over against death; so is the sinner over against the godly. And thus look upon all the works of the Most High; two and two, one against another. (Sir 33:14–15 RV)

The Two Ways functioned for the Jew as moral shorthand, and it was quickly adopted by the early Christian communities. By viewing life in the Spirit in terms of the Two Ways, the believer could easily relegate any aspect of his life and the paganism surrounding him to one of these two opposing camps. For example, wrath versus grace, retribution versus pardon, cursing versus blessing, fear versus trust, and life versus death. Believers easily grasped the idea that judgment, retribution, and greed were the way of death, just as pardon, forgiveness, and generosity were the way of life. And just as Paul taught that law was wrath and those in Christ were no longer under its curse, so too early believers quickly understood that the Mosaic law—the dead letter, the way of death—was opposed to the law of spirit—the living Word, the new law written on the heart, the way of life.[43]

---

42. Schaff, *Teaching of the Twelve*, 19–22.

43. Considering that the Two Ways discloses the opposing forces of law and grace so clearly, it is curious that Reformed theology attempts to conflate the two by teaching that the Ten Commandments remain a rule of life for those in Christ, in gratitude for salvation—or, as it is frequently summarized by Calvinists: guilt, grace, gratitude (See *Heidelberg Catechism*, 91, 115; also Berkhof, 614–15). Calvinists must specify the Ten Commandments, since the remainder of the Law is ceremonial and was abrogated by Jesus' atonement. Thus, Calvinists divide the Law into applicable and non-applicable parts. But it is doubtful that Paul would have concurred with such a division. F. F. Bruce notes that this idea must be read into Paul's doctrine (Bruce, 192–93). More significant still is that it is a fruitless attempt to mix the unmixable—for the law and grace are mutually exclusive. The law is the dead letter, wrath, and judgment. Although the law has not "passed away," it remains solely for those under its curse, and not for those under grace (Matt 5:18–19). My first assigned paper in seminary (which I still have) was supposed to address "The Continuing Significance of the Mosaic Law." It was returned with its margins filled with terse corrections, reprimands, and a grade of C for daring to deny this fundamental teaching of Calvinism. My arguments then were inchoate.

Early Christian Life   45

The Two Ways provided an easy method of discerning whether any specific act or attitude was acceptable. All of life was either one or the other, and the disciple of Jesus must choose, since both paths cannot be followed simultaneously. Many centuries later, the Radical Reformers would recover the doctrine of the Two Ways.

After its initial pronouncement of the Two Ways, the *Didache* sets forth a litany of sinful conduct. These were taught universally in the congregations, even though some are not specified in the New Testament.

> Thou shalt not kill. Thou shalt not commit adultery; thou shalt not corrupt boys; thou shalt not commit fornication. Thou shalt not steal. Thou shalt not use witchcraft; thou shalt not practice sorcery. Thou shalt not procure abortion, nor shalt thou kill the new-born child. Thou shalt not covet thy neighbor's goods. Thou shalt not forswear thyself. Thou shalt not bear false witness. Thou shalt not speak evil; thou shalt not bear malice. Thou shalt not be double-minded nor double-tongued; for duplicity of tongue is a snare of death. Thy speech shall not be false, nor vain, but fulfilled by deed. Thou shalt not be covetous, nor rapacious, nor a hypocrite, nor malignant, nor haughty. Thou shalt not take evil counsel against thy neighbor. Thou shalt not hate any one, but some thou shalt rebuke and for some thou shalt pray, and some thou shalt love above thine own soul (or, life).[44]

Personal conduct included the way a believer earned his living. The *Apostolic Tradition*, or *Canons*, attributed to Hippolytus and written about 218 CE, describes the examination of those seeking baptism. All professions and trades were examined. Before baptism, believers abandoned careers as actors, pagan priests, magicians, prostitutes, charioteers, and gladiators or gladiatorial trainers. Soldiers already engaged in the military were baptized only if they refused to kill in the course of duty; but anyone seeking a military profession after becoming a Christian was to be thrown out of the ecclesia, for he had despised the gospel. Military constables, proconsuls and civil magistrates—anyone who wore the purple or held the sword by proxy—were also forbidden occupations. This list was not exhaustive, as the *Tradition* indicates at its conclusion. The Holy Spirit would instruct as needed.[45]

---

44. *Did.* 2.2–7.
45. Arnold, *The Early Christians*, 108–109.

The conversion of slaves presented a unique problem for the ecclesia.

> The slave, even of a heathen, was not admitted unless he promised to deserve his master's good-will by honest behaviour, and to abandon every practice which was incompatible with his Christian vow and confession of faith in the proffered salvation.... But even the master of a slave was inadmissible into, or incapable of remaining in, the Communion, unless he gave his slaves, of both sexes, an opportunity of abandoning personal impurity, and of entering into married life. All the moral philosophers and national economists of the day (and the Romans were in this practically and theoretically eminent) must have held this to be a most serious, if not unjustifiable, attack on the rights of property, ever most sacred in the eyes of the Romans, the divine right of the Sovereign Man.[46]

Believers assiduously applied the principles of the kingdom, and conscientiously examined their conduct. They were thankful for salvation and for each other, and hospitality provided an opportunity to express thanksgiving for salvation—perhaps, even unknowingly entertain angels (Heb 13:2). But here too they were equally circumspect. "Travelling brethren were hospitably looked after in every way for two or three days; if anyone then wished to stay longer he had to earn his own living, but the community procured him work. Christian vagabondage was not tolerated."[47] This was in keeping with the *Didache*, which stated,

> Let every one that comes in the name of the Lord be received, and then proving him ye shall know him; for ye shall have understanding right and left. If indeed he who comes is a wayfarer, help him as much as ye can; but he shall not remain with you longer than two or three days, unless there be necessity. If he wishes to settle among you, being a craftsman (artisan), let him work and eat (earn his living by work). But if he has not handicraft (trade), provide according to your understanding that no Christian shall live idle among you. And if he will not act thus he is a Christ-trafficker. Beware of such.[48]

Thus, we see that early Christians had the same instructions as we do today concerning normal Christian deportment, but they understood

---

46. Bunsen, 2:107.
47. Dobschutz, *The Apostolic Age*, 127.
48. *Did.* 12.1–5.

them differently and applied them more rigorously. They viewed the surrounding culture as being under the domination of Satan and opposed to life in the Spirit. They were more sensitive and more willing to examine and then dispense with any aspect of their daily lives if it so much as hinted at conflict with their professed faith—even at the loss of income, family, friends, or freedom.

Edward Gibbon takes a more cynical view, even while admitting their faith was superior. "The ancient Christians were animated by a contempt for their present existence, and by a just confidence of immortality, of which the doubtful and imperfect faith of modern ages cannot give us any adequate notion."[49]

They expected the imminent return of their Lord, and declared an impending judgment of the world by fire, when Jesus would return in the clouds to judge all mankind. The earth would be restored to its original, sinless perfection and splendor at the restoration of all things. Although this prediction made them appear ludicrous, the Roman authorities took note of its potential threat to the established order.

Destruction of the world by fire was an early and prominent Christian teaching, and it explains why the emperor Nero (ruled 54–68 CE) was able to use the Christians as scapegoats after the conflagration of Rome on July 19, 64 CE. But this by no means implies that Nero discovered those actually responsible for the fire.[50] The fire devastated ten of the fourteen sectors of the city, and blame was attached quickly to the Christians. Tacitus (*Ann.* 15.44) narrates the pogrom initiated after the fire:

---

49. Gibbon, 1:187.

50. In his book, *Die Brände Roms: Ein apokalyptisches Motiv in der antiken Historiographi*. (Hildesheim: G. Olms, 1991), Gerhard Baudy conjectures that terrorists fired the metropolis and that the Christians were persecuted because an apocalyptic prophecy had pronounced that July 19 of that year would be "the day of the Lord." Christians were waiting for the end of the world in their own lifetime and they saw themselves as judges executing God's will upon the imminent *parousia* of Christ. Since all Christians were longing for liberation through a great fire, Baudy suggests a prophet revealed the mysterious "day of the Lord" and gave the signal for the eschatological burning of the city. Now, it is undisputed that judgment by fire was common knowledge amongst Christians. Paul knows it (1 Cor 3:13, 15; 2 Thess 1:7–8). Peter states it clearly in his letter (2 Pet 3:7) written about that same year. But Dr. Baudy's hypothesis that a Christian prophet notified believers that the day of the Lord was expected on July 19 is unsubstantiated, as is his suggestion that terrorists set fire to Rome to speed its arrival. Tacitus implies the rumors were correct: Nero ordered the fire. Suetonius states it as fact (*Nero* 38).

> But all human efforts, all the lavish gifts of the emperor, and the propitiations of the gods, did not banish the sinister belief that the conflagration was the result of an order. Consequently, to get rid of the report, Nero fastened the guilt and inflicted the most exquisite tortures on a class hated for their abominations, called Christians by the populace. Christus, from whom the name had its origin, suffered the extreme penalty during the reign of Tiberius at the hands of one of our procurators, Pontius Pilatus, and a most mischievous superstition, thus checked for the moment, again broke out not only in Judaea, the first source of the evil, but even in Rome, where all things hideous and shameful from every part of the world find their centre and become popular. Accordingly, an arrest was first made of all who pleaded guilty; then, upon their information, an immense multitude was convicted, not so much of the crime of firing the city, as of hatred against mankind. Mockery of every sort was added to their deaths. Covered with the skins of beasts, they were torn by dogs and perished, or were nailed to crosses, or were doomed to the flames and burnt, to serve as a nightly illumination, when daylight had expired.
>
> Nero offered his gardens for the spectacle, and was exhibiting a show in the circus, while he mingled with the people in the dress of a charioteer or stood aloft on a car. Hence, even for criminals who deserved extreme and exemplary punishment, there arose a feeling of compassion; for it was not, as it seemed, for the public good, but to glut one man's cruelty, that they were being destroyed.[51]

Schaff adds that

> Christianity was novel, detached from any particular nationality, and aiming at universal dominion. . . . Their Jewish origin, their indifference to politics and public affairs, their abhorrence of heathen customs, were construed into an "*odium generis humani*" and this made an attempt on their part to destroy the city sufficiently plausible to justify a verdict of guilty. An infuriated mob does not stop to reason, and is as apt to run mad as an individual.[52]

The Great Fire of Rome in 64 was a crucial moment for Christianity. Although Christians had been able to avoid detection by their appearance as a sect of Judaism, or one of the many confraternities, Ramsay notes, "Gradually people began to realize that Christianity meant a social

---

51. Tacitus, 168.
52. Schaff, *History of the Christian Church*, 1:381.

revolution, that it did not mean to take its place alongside of the other religions, but to destroy them."[53] Once apparent, Christians were no longer safe, as James Orr explains:

> There were special features about Christianity which, from a Roman standpoint, made tolerance impossible. Christianity was not a *national* religion. The sentiment of antiquity respected the gods of other nations; but Christianity appeared rather in the light of a revolt against the ancient faith from which it sprang, and had no national character of its own. It had no visible deity or temple, and to the popular mind, seemed a species of *atheism*. Specially, it could not fail to be seen that, with its exclusive claims, it struck at the very existence of the Roman state religion. If its precepts were admitted, the state religion would be overthrown. The more earnest men were, therefore, to maintain or revive the prestige of the established system, the more determinedly must they oppose this new superstition. The irreconcilability of Christianity with the established religion came naturally to its sharpest point in the refusal of Christians to offer at the shrine of the Emperor. This was an act of disobedience in a vital respect, which could not be passed over.[54]

"So long as men did not break the law and paid official respect to the established gods," Biggs adds, "more especially to the divinity of Caesar, they might worship what they pleased."[55] But the divinity of the emperor was abhorrent to the early believers.[56] Nothing so offended the Christian conscience as the cult of the emperor. "The most trifling mark of respect to the national worship he considered as a direct homage yielded to the daemon, and as an act of rebellion against the majesty of God," notes Gibbon.[57]

> The Genius was, if not the man himself, at any rate the man's own god, a notion which the Christian, though he would have found no great difficulty in the idea of a guardian angel, could not possibly accept. He could allow himself to swear by the Health of Augustus, but to take oath by, or in any way to acknowledge, the Fortune or

53. Ramsay, 130.
54. Orr, 13–14.
55. Bigg, 27.
56. Deissmann, 347–71. The imperial cult infringed on Christian terminology and ideas, and accommodation was impossible in the early years. Deissmann discusses this subject at length.
57 Gibbon, 1:184.

the Genius of the Emperor he regarded as flat idolatry. But this was the most common form of oath, and this acknowledgement was pressed upon him at every turn. There were two remarkable occasions on which it was exceedingly difficult to escape. At every dinner-party, as soon as the first course was removed, and the toasts began, the statuettes of the Lares were brought in from the Atrium or hall of the house and placed upon the table, and libations were poured out to the deities of the family and to the Genius of Augustus, very much as we might drink to Church and State, and propose the health of the entertainer. The Christian was obliged therefore either to refuse all invitations from his heathen neighbours, to commit an overt act of disaffection which might cost him his life, or to do what his stricter brethren would regard as apostasy.[58]

Arnold points out that the early believers "abhorred and attacked this mixture of the religious and the patriotic. . . . They declared openly that emperors could only believe in Christ if they were not emperors—as if Christians could ever be emperors."[59]

After Roman authorities realized that Christians would not offer sacrifice to the genius of the Emperor, this alone provided a quick and ready test of true allegiance. Typically, after arrest, the authorities compelled Christians, on threat of death, to renounce Jesus and burn a bit of incense before the image of the Emperor. That small act alone was sufficient to earn immediate release. Those who declined, in most cases, were summarily executed in a variety of ways. But it was not always a simple matter for the magistrate.

The letter from Pliny the Younger, governor of Bithynia-Pontus, to the emperor Trajan in 112 CE furnishes evidence of both the obstinacy of the Christians and Pliny's frustration with this "extravagant superstition."

Pliny Secundus to Emperor Trajan:

It is with me, sir, an established custom to refer to you all matters on which I am in doubt. Who, indeed, is better able, either to direct my scruples or to instruct my ignorance? I have never been present at trials of Christians and consequently do not know for what reasons, or how far, punishment is usually inflicted or inquiry made in their case. Nor have my hesitations been slight:

---

58. Bigg, 16.
59. Arnold, *The Early Christians*, 23.

as to whether any distinction of age should be made, or persons however tender in years should be viewed as differing in no respect from the full-grown: whether pardon should be accorded to repentance, or he who has once been a Christian should gain nothing by having ceased to be one: whether the very profession itself if unattended by crime, or else the crimes necessarily attaching to the profession, should be made the subject of punishment.

Meanwhile, in the case of those who have been brought before me in the character of Christians, my course has been as follows: I put it to themselves whether they were or were not Christians. To such as professed that they were, I put the inquiry a second and a third time, threatening them with the supreme penalty. Those who persisted, I ordered to execution. For, indeed, I could not doubt, whatever might be the nature of that which they professed, that their pertinacity, at any rate, and inflexible obstinacy, ought to be punished. There were others afflicted with like madness, with regard to whom, as they were Roman citizens, I made a memorandum that they were to be sent for judgment to Rome. Soon, the very handling of this matter causing, as often happens, the area of the charge to spread, many fresh examples occurred. An anonymous paper was put forth containing the names of many persons. Those who denied that they either were or had been Christians, upon their calling on the gods after me, and upon their offering wine and incense before your statue, which for this purpose I had ordered to be introduced in company with the images of the gods, moreover upon their reviling Christ—none of which things it is said can such as are really and truly Christians be compelled to do—these I deemed it proper to dismiss. Others named by the informer admitted that they were Christians, and then shortly afterwards denied it, adding that they had been Christians, but had ceased to be so, some three years, some many years, more than one of them as much as twenty years, before. All these, too, not only honoured your image and the effigies of the gods, but also reviled Christ. They affirmed, however, that this had been the sum, whether of their crime or their delusion; they had been in the habit of meeting together on a stated day, before sunrise, and of offering in turns a form of invocation to Christ, as to a god; also of binding themselves by an oath, not for any guilty purpose, but not to commit thefts, or robberies, or adulteries, not to break their word, not to repudiate deposits when called upon; these ceremonies having been gone through, they had been in the habit of separating, and again meeting together for the purpose of taking food—food, that is, of an ordinary and innocent kind. They had, however, ceased from doing even this, after my edict, in which, following your orders, I had forbidden the existence of Fraternities. This made me think it all the more necessary to inquire, even by torture, of two maid-servants, who were styled deaconesses, what the truth was. I could discover nothing else than a vicious and extravagant superstition: consequently, having adjourned the inquiry, I have had recourse to your counsels. Indeed, the matter seemed to me a proper one for consultation, chiefly on account of the number of persons imperilled. For many of all ages and all ranks, ay, and of both sexes, are being called, and will be called, into danger. Nor are cities only permeated by the contagion of this superstition, but villages and country parts as well; yet it seems possible to stop it and cure it. It is in truth sufficiently evident that the temples, which were almost entirely deserted, have begun to be frequented, that the customary religious rites which had long been interrupted are being resumed, and that there is a sale for the food of sacrificial beasts, for which hitherto very few buyers indeed could be found. From all this it is easy to form an opinion as to the great number of persons who may be reclaimed, if only room be granted for penitence.

Trajan to Pliny Secundus:

You have followed the right mode of procedure, my dear Secundus in investigating the cases of those who had been brought before you as Christians. For, indeed, it is not possible to establish any universal rule, possessing as it were a fixed form. These people should not be searched for; if they are informed against and convicted they should be punished; yet, so that he who shall deny being a Christian, and shall make this plain in action, that is by worshipping our gods, even though suspected on account of his past conduct, shall obtain pardon by his penitence. Anonymous informations, however, ought not to be allowed a standing in any kind of charge; a course which would not only form the worst of precedents, but which is not in accordance with the spirit of our time.[60]

Trajan's rescript was reasonable. Although it is obvious Pliny and the emperor are discussing a standing procedure, and not a new order or attitude,[61] Trajan is evidently reticent to give Pliny anything more than general guidelines in dealing with this movement. Foremost in Trajan's mind is his determination to reject the methods used by his predeces-

---

60. Lewis, 377–80.
61. Robertson, 77.

sors based on anonymous accusers—the hated *delatores*.[62] His reaction clearly indicates that Christianity was still little more than a suspicious movement—hardly an overwhelming threat to the security of the republic. Trajan assumes that Pliny will determine for himself a reasonable course of action.

However, Trajan's successors were both less measured and less reasonable. Over the succeeding century and a half, as persecutions erupted in the provinces from time to time, here and there, many Christians succumbed to the threats of torture or death and denounced their faith to save their lives. After failing that test, the spiritual state of these "lapsed" (*lapsi*) became an increasingly important problem for the ecclesiae. Initially, the spiritual state of the lapsed was a local issue, but as the ranks of the lapsed swelled, those in positions of oversight in the various congregations sought to create a uniform policy to deal with them. By that time, the organization of the ecclesiae had changed significantly enough to provide the means in that effort.

---

62. *Delatores* (anonymous accusers) had been used widely by emperors in times past. By requiring that accusations be stated formally, the accuser was in legal jeopardy, should the accusation prove false.

4

The Ecclesia Changes

Before Paul sailed for Jerusalem and into subsequent Roman captivity, he reminded the Ephesian elders at Miletus (Acts 20:34–35) that they were to shepherd the congregation by the power of the Holy Spirit. He admonished them to carry on in vigilance, just as he had done—that is, following his example.

He ominously predicted that fierce wolves would attack the ecclesiae. "From among your own selves shall men arise, speaking perverse things, to draw away the disciples after them" (Acts 20:30 ASV). Some of these perversions that Paul had foreseen arising from within the ecclesiae are set forth in the letters to the seven churches of the Apocalypse (Rev 2:1–3:22). But perversions come in all sorts of clothing. Certainly they may appear as grossly false doctrine, and may even lead to sin; but they may appear also in reasonable and attractive garb.

Paul's prediction was ultimately fulfilled 391 CE when the emperor Theodosius, by formal edict, forbade all worship of the heathen gods and declared Christianity the Roman state religion—thereby uniting grace with wrath. But that apostasy was merely the culmination of a series of events—a cascade that began three hundred years earlier from two separate directions. It was the reactions to the twin attacks of heresy and persecution that eventually altered the spiritual foundation and organization of the ecclesiae. Changes in its organization permitted and hastened the blending of Christianity with the pagan culture encircling it, inevitably resulting in apostate doctrine, and bequeathing to us the institutional church in its variety of conceptions, opinions, and creeds.

Heresy drew disciples away and persecution scattered them. For those whose task it was to shepherd, it was natural, perhaps, to seek any method that might prevent the dismemberment of the congregations, even if those methods were questionable. Their reaction was similar to that of wagon trains heading west in nineteenth-century America, which quickly formed a circle to protect the party when attacked. Yet, when the wagons of the ecclesiae formed a circle, the prophets were left outside.

To the ecclesiae of the first century, the idea of a false prophet was constituted by the pretence of being a prophet—"having received divine revelations when that was not the case."[1] The prophets of the first century were obliged to submit to the criticism of their fellow Christians, and were warned against unnatural excitement and the "confusion of their own thought and fancies with what was given to them by the Spirit."[2]

Gore elaborates:

> In the *Didache* the true prophet is distinguished from the false "by his fruits", i.e. by his genuine poverty and disinterestedness and by his orthodoxy. So far he is subject to the testing of the Church. But once his true prophetic inspiration is accepted, it becomes a sin against the Holy Ghost to judge him. The remarkable feature in the prophets in the *Didache* is that, like those at Antioch in the Acts, they become, wherever they appear, the chief ministers of worship, no less than of teaching. They hold, with the less defined figures of apostle and teacher, the first rank in the church hierarchy.[3]

As we observed in chapter 2, the independent ecclesiae were originally bound together and shepherded by the twofold prophetic and local ministries. The local ministry bound the individual members of the congregation together and the prophetic ministry bound the various ecclesiae together. But, between the writing of the *Didache* and Irenaeus (c. 70–180 CE), a revolution in the organization of the church occurred—with little to no resistance. The local ministry eclipsed the authority of the prophetic ministry.

Restrictions on the prophetic ministry were imposed rapidly, but the actual beginning of this change is obscure. We know that the *Epistle of Barnabas* (written c. 70–80 CE) is free from the urgent precepts that mark Clement, Ignatius and other writers of the organized church, who were ordering submission to the presbyter and the bishop.[4] As Gore notes, "It is clear that at the time of the *Shepherd of Hermas* [written c. 90–100 CE] the prophet did not hold anything like the position which he held in the

1. Selwyn, *The Christian Prophets*, 50.
2. Ibid., 49–50.
3. Gore, *Church and the Ministry*, 355.
4. Selwyn, *The Christian Prophets*, 79.

Didache. No doubt the abundance of pretenders to inspiration made it plain that prophecy, even if an abiding endowment of the Church, was a rare one and not intended for the Church to depend upon for a supply of her chief ministers."[5] Gore's "abundance of pretenders"—a fact admitted by Tertullian and others—does not prove that true prophecy was rare, but it certainly provides an incentive to restrict prophecy in the ecclesia.

What is also unclear is why a single bishop was beginning to be elevated by many congregations to leadership above the local session of elders before the end of the first century. Gore readily admits no clear evidence exists: "there is considerable doubt how the rule of the single bishop in each church actually came about."[6] Did the need for restrictions on the prophetic ministry play a part, or was it something else entirely?

Philip Moxom comments on this period:

> At first the terms "bishop" and "presbyter" were interchangeable; then the bishop was called also "presbyter," though the presbyter was not called "bishop." The title, previously common to all the presbyters, was thus appropriated to one. This appropriation, however, could scarcely have taken place much before the end of the first or the early years of the second century; certainly this is true of the Christian communities among the heathen. "As late as the year 70," says J. B. Lightfoot, "no distinct signs of the episcopal government had appeared in Gentile Christendom." Before the middle of the second century, however, we find the office of bishop quite clearly defined. In the letters of Ignatius (110–117 A.D.) the episcopate appears in so advanced a stage of development as to indicate that the development had been going on in the East for some years. This development was perhaps stimulated among Jewish Christians by the fall of Jerusalem and the loss of a visible centre. But in all Christian communities the need of some unifying force in organization and administration was early felt.[7]

The attempt to eclipse the prophetic ministry did not go completely unchecked. Montanism[8] was a reaction to both the recession of the prophetic ministry and the emergence of a single man as shepherd. It made its appearance in the middle of the second century in Phrygia, where

---

5. Gore, *Church and Ministry*, 356.

6. Gore, *Orders and Unity*, 129.

7. Moxom, 68.

8. Bigg, Duchesne, and Schaff provide extensive background and details of the movement.

enthusiasm had made a home, and is best described as an outbreak of prophetic mysticism.[9] Montanists contended that the prophets were being suppressed by the local ministry and that the church had fallen into grave error—had become unholy. As Louis Duchesne points out, "Both tradition and custom had consecrated the right of prophets to arouse Christians in the name of the Lord. The Didache and the New Testament both show what a prominent place prophecy held in the life of the early church."[10] Montanists claimed that the church had turned aside from direction by the Holy Spirit and teaching through the prophets, and that the bishops, whose authority the Montanists rejected, had usurped that position in the congregations.

Montanism was the first schism to confront the church.[11] Although much of its history may be the exaggeration, calumny, or slander of its opponents, it is significant that its most famous adherent was Tertullian. Montanus—according to some traditions, a former priest of Cybele[12]—disappeared quickly, and little is known about him, except that he attracted attention through bizarre and ecstatic proclamations and claimed to speak the very words of God through the Paraclete.

The two major prophets of the movement were Prisca and Maximilla—both women, as were most of the movement's prophets. According to Montanist prophets, the Paraclete was manifesting himself anew. It announced that the heavenly Jerusalem would soon descend on a plain in Phrygia between the towns of Pepuza and Tymion.[13] In preparation for this momentous event, its followers dissolved marriages, cut all earthly and family ties, and shared in a community of goods. The failure of the prediction did not dissuade the followers. But it should be noted that prophesies of the imminent return of Christ were not unique to Montanism.[14]

9. Bigg, 185.
10. Duchesne, 1:197–98.
11. Bigg, 187.
12. Duchesne, 1:196.
13. Ibid., 1:197.
14. Duchesne notes: "This Montanist Exodus did not stand alone. Hippolytus, (In Dan. iv. i8), mentions a similar event in his own day. A Syrian bishop led out a host of Christians, men, women, and children into the desert to meet Christ. In the end these poor dupes were arrested as brigands. Another bishop, this time in Pontus, predicted the end of the world during the current year; his people sold their cattle, and left their land untilled to prepare for the great day. In the 3rd century, a prophetess of Cappadocia is

Montanism spread quickly, leaving some congregations totally abandoned in its wake, as converts flocked to the new movement. Duchesne explains the reaction to the ecstasy of the movement:

> Some of [the Christian churches] had been in existence for nearly a century or more, and had grown accustomed to live an ordinary life with no special pre-occupation as to the end of all things. They soon met the prophets with the objection that their proceedings were contrary to custom. In the Old Testament, as in the New, prophets had never spoken in a state of ecstasy. The communication which, by their means, was established between God and their hearers, had not hindered them from preserving their own individuality. They spoke in the name of God, but it was they themselves who spoke. In the case of Montanus and his prophetesses, the Paraclete himself was heard, just as in certain pagan sanctuaries, the gods were heard to speak directly, by the mouth of pythonesses. "The man himself is a lyre," said the inspired voice, "and I am the bow which causes him to vibrate. . . . I am not an angel, nor a messenger. . . . I am the Lord, the Almighty." . . . This seemed unusual, and an abuse, and reprehensible.[15]

Bigg states:

> The appearance of the new sect filled Asia Minor with anger and alarm. . . . For the first time it was openly maintained by Christians that the Catholic Church was not holy and did not really believe in the teaching of the Spirit. The authority of the bishops was set at naught, and an ignorant band of Phrygian peasants was flouting the intelligence, the learning, and even the religious character of their pastors and masters, and this at a time when the unity of the Church was absolutely necessary to its existence. . . . The only point upon which it lay obviously open to attack was its notion of Inspiration, a word which never has been and never can be accurately defined. What is a True Prophet?[16]

The most remarkable feature of Montanism was its moral rigor.[17] It was a puritanical attempt to call believers back to a strict moral life. As a Montanist, Tertullian went so far as to claim that whatever was not

---

mentioned, who started an immense multitude en route for Jerusalem." Duchesne, 1:197 n. 1.

15. Ibid., 1:198.
16. Bigg, 187.
17. Ibid., 190.

expressly *permitted* in Scripture was forbidden, and that the time had come for the stricter Christian law to be revealed. Yet, Montanists taught that the Holy Spirit could not be bound to a specific canon of writings. According to Bigg,

> It was a natural consequence of the authority allowed to the prophets that the Montanists did not regard the Bible as complete. This was evidently the main question involved; and, as the New Prophets claimed authority to deal with both doctrine and discipline, it is also evident that the whole future of the Church was imperiled. But the question is also one of infinite difficulty. All Scripture is inspired by God. May we invert this proposition and say that every utterance inspired by God is equivalent to Scripture? The Holy Spirit guides the Church into all truth. But does He impart new truths, or does He merely bestow a clearer understanding of the old? . . . All parties agreed that there had been false prophets, and that other false prophets were yet to come. But what were the tests by which the false could be distinguished from the true?[18]

Many of the writings that were read in the various congregations, or in private, were being systematically culled, as the church codified the New Testament. Books like *Shepherd*, *Barnabas*, the *Didache*, *Enoch*, and others were no longer considered equal to those books that comprise our New Testament—not because they were not inspired, but because they were not written by the original apostles. They were not banned until the fourth century; instead, they were simply considered of lesser spiritual value. Although no longer read in the congregations, they were permitted for private reading and devotion.

But the Montanists held that Scripture was not complete and that prophecy was equal to Scripture. This shift alarmed the local ministry. In former times, prophets were judged against the established teaching of the Apostles. From this point forward, prophets became suspect by merely claiming to be prophets.

The Montanist movement eventually made its way to Rome, where it was declared not only a schism, but heresy, and its followers were excommunicated by several Asiatic synods before 193.[19] Bigg describes the fervor with which the Montanists were castigated:

---

18. Ibid., 194.
19. Ibid., 188.

> The most furious charges were levelled against the sect. . . . Before the end of the second century it was currently believed that the Montanists celebrated their Eucharist with the flesh and blood of a murdered child. The Catholics themselves had been charged with this horrible crime by the heathen, and now they were neither ashamed nor afraid to assert that some Christians were guilty of it.[20]

After Christianity joined with the state, Montanists were systematically persecuted by Constantine and, later, by Theodosius, who declared Montanism illegal and eradicated its adherents by fire and the sword. According to Bigg, "The so-called seventh canon of the Council of Constantinople affirms that they are not to be regarded as Christians at all, and a glance at the index of the Theodosian Code will reveal a number of cruel laws directed against this harmless and maligned sect, whose main offence was that they were foolish enough to prefer a prophet to a bishop."[21]

The significance of Montanism was not its heretical teachings or even the unusual behavior of its prophets. Rather, it was the attempt to reestablish the prophetic ministry. The crucial question of the moment was, who was in charge? Was it the prophetic ministry or the local ministry in the hands of the emerging bishops—the episcopacy?

Gore disagrees with this assessment of events. He says, "Even an opponent of the false prophets of Montanism recognized that prophecy must continue in the whole Church to the end."[22] However, it is one thing to recognize an idea theoretically and quite another to permit it. According to Gore and others, the Montanist prophets were rejected by the church "especially on account of the ecstatic and irrational character of their supposed gifts. . . . Their rejection involved no slight at all on the gift of prophecy and no denial of its claims."[23] But for Gore to insist that prophecy "must continue in the whole Church to the end" and that the rejection of Montanism was "no slight at all and no denial of its claims" implies that prophecy was at least still anticipated by the church. That is simply not the case. Prophecy had been so restricted by the middle of the second century that it was no longer important or anticipated. And, to settle the

---

20. Ibid., 188.
21. Ibid., 189.
22. Gore, *Church and Ministry*, 355.
23. Ibid.

issue, prophecy began to be defined as the *teaching of the bishop*,[24] which further undermined the validity of the prophetic ministry.

Gore's position is that today, as then, "the genuine gift [of prophecy] has become exceedingly rare"[25] and, because it is rare, it has ceased to be usual. We will examine Gore's position in chapter 8. At this point, however, we must ask, was the "recession" of the gift of prophecy *the cause* or *the consequence* of the rise of episcopacy? That is to say, was the gift of prophecy rare because it had been withdrawn or because it had been eclipsed?

Selwyn observes that "self-assertion, exaggeration, and irregularity may probably have roused the orderly sense of the bishops to oppose the Prophets. This led to a schism; the schism was magnified into heresy; the 'heresy' was eventually quenched and the prophetic gift was cut off and ceased, appearing only sporadically in the succeeding centuries."[26]

Initially, a collegiate session of elders had possessed oversight of the local ecclesia. But, by the end of the first century, a new form of government appeared in the hand of one man. In place of the twofold prophetic and local ministry, a *threefold local ministry*, consisting of a bishop, elders, and deacons, assumed leadership. The prophetic ministry was eclipsed and a single man was eventually elevated by the collegiate session of elders to the superior position of bishop. The sole voice of protest against this revolution was Montanism. This transition of authority was accomplished by 250 CE, under the firm direction of three key architects: Ignatius, Irenaeus, and Cyprian.

Lindsay states: "Whatever paths led to the change in the ministry whereby the rule was transferred from a college of elders without a president to a college with a president, when once the change was made the power of the *episcopus* grew rapidly; and one source of this increase of authority lay in the fact that he was always the administrator of the property of the local church."[27]

The prophetic ministry, which had been more esteemed and superior to the local ministry, became *subject to the local office bearers*. This imposed subjection did not come through judgment by the congregation of the prophet's message and fruit, as had been the practice. Instead, the

---

24. Lindsay, 227–28.
25. Gore, *Church and Ministry*, 355.
26. Selwyn, *The Christian Prophets*, 16–17.
27. Lindsay, 209–210.

test of a true prophet became *whether that prophet was obedient to the local officers—obedient to both their authority and doctrine*. Both Clement and Ignatius "threw their weight into the scale of the organisation on episcopal lines, to which the prophetic order, such as it was, tended to present a rival and even antagonistic attitude."[28] Ignatius's command was "obey the Bishop and the presbytery with an undistracted mind."[29]

Lindsay sees this revolution at the local level as fitting and necessary, given the circumstances. "One man can take a firmer grip of things. Divided responsibility continually means varying counsels. What is the business of many is often the work of none."[30] Hence, Ignatius encouraged an undivided front by means of a single bishop during times of crisis and persecution.

By the time Ignatius wrote his letters on the way to martyrdom (c. 108–117 CE), the threefold local ministry was established widely, although not universally. Ignatius encouraged the congregations to adopt the threefold ministry and "do nothing without the bishop."[31] Later still, Cyprian could state: "The bishop is in the church, and the church in the bishop, and if anyone is not with the bishop he is not in the church."[32]

Lightfoot quotes Jerome (c. 347–420), who ascribed this change in church polity to preservation; but Jerome's argument would appear to be a somewhat simplistic, fourth-century justification.

> "Before factions were introduced into religion by the prompting of the devil" the churches were governed by a council of elders. "But as soon as each man began to consider those whom he had baptized to belong to himself and not to Christ, it was decided throughout the world that one elected from among the elders should be placed over the rest, so that the care of the church should devolve on him and the seeds of schism be removed."[33]

Selwyn points out that "it does appear that we possess certain traces of *a disappearing prophetic mode of thought*, a prophetic way of viewing events, a prophetic treatment of O.T. Scripture and uncanonical writings,

---

28. Selwyn, *The Christian Prophets*, 12.

29. Ibid., 12. Selwyn notes that the term "undistracted" is a "delicate hit" at the ecstasy of the prophets.

30. Lindsay 206.

31. Ibid., 193.

32. Benson, 37.

33. Lightfoot, *The Christian Ministry*, 39.

which existed down to the year 70 AD, and had ceased to exist by 140."[34] He adds: "The Churches were compelled by the divine law of their being to decide between Prophecy and Order."[35] Gore agrees that order was essential. "The prophets of the *Didache* at least afford us evidence that the continuity of the Church tradition could not have been allowed to rest upon prophets, nor an ambulatory prophetic ministry to become permanent in the Church, without widespread disorder."[36]

But how did this widespread disorder ever begin? What had become of the gift of discernment and the prohibition of false prophets by the assemblies, as was the common practice in the first century? Gore is incorrect in his assessment. The ecclesia is built upon the prophetic ministry. It was never a temporary expedient. The prophetic ministry is needed most in times of trial.

At its core, something far more familiar and common was afoot. Direction by the Holy Spirit through the prophets was disturbing for the local ministry in the late first century. It was unpredictable and often untidy. More importantly, it demanded that each ecclesia, and even every believer, know the Spirit of Messiah well enough to discern false doctrine and turn a deaf ear to it. The Twelve, Paul, Barnabas, Timothy, and the rest were all dead and the congregations were adrift in a hostile world of persecution and heresy. The local ministry wanted *consistency* and *predictability*. Consistency and predictability always require less effort and less individual responsibility. They are tidy and comfortable. Consistency and predictability are equated with, and often mistaken for, truth.

The simple solution—the solution that maintained order, eliminated the unpredictable, and required less effort—was to prohibit the prophets and elevate one man in each congregation who would teach consistent, uniform, and uncontested doctrine.

In short, regulation was needed.

---

34. Selwyn, *St. Luke the Prophet*, 271.
35. Selwyn, *The Christian Prophets*, ix.
36. Gore, *Church and Ministry*, 255.

5

The Rise of the Episcopacy

As we observed in the last chapter, the authority of the prophetic ministry was restricted, and eventually eclipsed, by the authority of the local ministry. But the local ministry itself was quickly exchanged for the episcopacy—that form of ecclesiastical government with a bishop (ἐπίσκοπος) elevated to a position above, and superior in authority to, a session of elders, or the local ministry.

Ernst von Dobschutz remarks that "insistence on fixed regulations is perhaps the most outstanding feature of this late period"—by which he means the period from Clement to the death of Ignatius, or about 80–117 CE. "Reliance on the free development of the Spirit had disappeared; it was sought to regulate everything. . . . Free utterances of the Spirit have become suspicious in their doctrinal aspect. Teaching and speaking, till then open to all, became confined to the clergy, whose office was entrusted only to reliable people and afforded a guarantee of the right tradition of sound, pure doctrine (2 Tim. ii. 2)."[1]

In the formative years of the episcopacy, congregations directly elected one man as bishop from their collegiate sessions of elders. But it quickly became evident to those in authority that democratic power, in the unchecked hands of the local congregation, permitted the elevation of *any* individual to the office of bishop. Thus, those who favored an ordered and uniform ecclesia sought to limit that selection to ensure orthodoxy. It was the theory of *apostolic succession* that provided the means to its achievement. Statements by Clement and Irenaeus (180–200 CE) were cited as the legal basis for apostolic succession. Since Lindsay has proved that the statement by Irenaeus actually concerns the succession of truth

---

1. Dobschutz, *Christian Life in the Primitive Church*, 281.

in doctrine,[2] and not apostolic succession, as it is classically defined, we'll restrict our examination to the citation from Clement.

Clement's statement appears in his Letter to the Corinthians (*1 Clem.* 44), written about 96 CE. It is the sole basis for the idea of apostolic succession. He writes: "And our Apostles knew through our Lord Jesus Christ that there would be strife over the name of the bishop's office. For this cause therefore, having received complete foreknowledge, they appointed the aforesaid persons, and afterwards gave a further injunction that if they should fall asleep, other approved men should succeed to their ministration."[3] This supposed event is known to Irenaeus as the "second ordinances" of the apostles—later decrees or injunctions by the remaining Apostles, and unknown to history, apart from the testimony of Irenaeus, Clement, and Eusebius.[4]

But Clement's statement may not mean all that succeeding generations hoped and claimed for it, as William Sanday observes:

> St. Clement is insisting here on the regular and responsible appointment of the Corinthian presbyters. He does not hint in any way at a transmission of powers. The [other approved men] are not, as some translations of Clement's language might lead us to suppose, placed on the direct line of descent from the Apostles. When we think of the importance of prophecy and the activity of prophets in the Apostolic age, it is very improbable that all who held office or dignity in the Church were appointed to it directly by Apostles in either the wider or the narrower sense. The state of things described by St. Clement is just what would be natural. Nominations to office would be made by an Apostle, if one was

---

2. "Irenaeus proposed to give to this old and much used method of finding out what were the primary and fixed verities of the Christian faith the sanction of an ecclesiastical usage. Here we meet for the first time, outside the Roman Church, the thought of a succession from the apostles in the office-bearers of the local churches; but it is a very different thing from the 'gigantic figment' of an Apostolic Succession which dominates the Anglican and is a law in the Roman Church of the present day. It is meant to be a simple and clear way to find out what the real faith of the Church is in a time of more than usual perplexity. This is evident from the application Irenaeus makes of his principle, and it is also clear from the manner in which Tertullian, who adopts the principle, illustrates the use to be made of it" (Lindsay, 224). For a full discussion, see Lindsay, 223–29.

3. Sanday, 71.

4. Lightfoot, *The Christian Ministry*, 34–35.

available, if not by those whom the Church most trusted. But in all cases the assent of the Church was required.[5]

As Selwyn points out, hidden beneath the conception of apostolic succession is a certain veneration of the elders that had its origin in Judaism:

> One of the last verses of [Joshua] is very instructive to Jewish-Christians of the time, and it is this: "And Israel worshipped the Lord all the days of [Joshua] and all the days of the elders, as many as had lived out the time with [Joshua] and as many as had seen all the works of the Lord which he had done to Israel" [Joshua 24:31]. The effect of this passage on the early Church would be to increase the veneration in which the Christian elders were held, but also, and especially, to cause all the new Israel of God to persevere in the ancient worship of Temple and Synagogue throughout the lifetime of *the elders who had seen the Lord*. The effect of this veneration is discernible as late even as the time of Irenaeus, long after the time at which the original basis of it in the Book of [Joshua] had been forgotten.[6]

This succession of elders in Joshua was transformed into the idea of apostolic succession—and the concept was enticing, for it appeared to provide the security of traditional doctrine through the successive laying on of hands, even while it restricted authority to a select group within the ecclesiae. Ignatius (c. 35–117 CE) strongly supported it. On his way to martyrdom, in 117 CE, he wrote to the Trallians:

> When ye are obedient to the bishop as to Jesus Christ, it is evident to me that ye are living not after men but after Jesus Christ.... It is therefore necessary, even as your wont is, that ye should do nothing without the bishop; but be ye obedient also to the presbytery, as to the apostles.... And those likewise who are deacons of the mysteries of Jesus Christ must please all men in all ways. For they are not deacons of meats and drinks but servants of the church of God. It is right therefore that they should beware of blame as of fire. In like manner let all men respect the deacons as Jesus Christ, even as they should respect the bishop as being a type of the Father and the presbyters as the council of God and as the college of apostles. Apart from these there is not even the name of a church.... This will surely be, if ye be not puffed up and if ye be inseparable from

---

5. Sanday, 72.

6. Selwyn, *St. Luke the Prophet*, 62–63.

Jesus Christ, and from the bishop and from the ordinances of the Apostles. He that is within the sanctuary is clean; but he that is without the sanctuary is not clean, that is, he that doeth aught without the bishop and presbytery and deacons, this man is not clean in his conscience.... Fare ye well in Jesus Christ, submitting yourselves to the bishop as to the commandment, and likewise also to the presbytery.[7]

To the Philadelphians, he wrote:

> For as many as are of God and of Jesus Christ, they are with the bishop; and as many as shall repent and enter into the unity of the Church, these also shall be of *God*.... Be ye careful therefore to observe one eucharist (for there is one flesh of our Lord Jesus Christ and one cup unto union in His blood; there is one altar, as there is one bishop, together with the presbytery and the deacons my fellow-servants), that whatsoever ye do, ye may do it after God. ... Do nothing without the bishop.[8]

And to the Smyrnaeans, he wrote:

> Shun divisions, as the beginning of evils. Do ye all follow your bishop, as Jesus Christ followed the Father, and the presbytery as the apostles; and to the deacons pay respect, as to God's commandment. Let no man do aught of things pertaining to the church apart from the bishop. Let that be held a valid eucharist which is under the bishop or one to whom he shall have committed it. Wheresoever the bishop shall appear, there let the people be; even as where Jesus may be, there is the universal church. It is not lawful apart from the bishop either to baptize or to hold a love-feast; but whatever he shall approve, this is well-pleasing also to God; that everything which ye do may be sure and valid. It is good to recognize God and the bishop. He that honoureth the bishop is honoured of God; he that doeth aught without the knowledge of the bishop rendereth service to the devil.[9]

As Montgomery Hitchcock notes, both Irenaeus and Tertullian concurred with this conception of office and authority:

> The unbroken line of bishops in the Church, Irenaeus repeatedly says, is the test and safeguard of apostolic doctrine. Apostolic de-

---

7. Ign. *Trall.* 2, 3, 7, 13, ed. Lightfoot, *The Apostolic Fathers*, 147–49.
8. Ign. *Phld.* 3, 4, 7.
9. Ign. *Smyrn.* 8.

scent is the guarantee of the uniformity of belief. It is more reasonable that the truth should be found among those who can trace back their ministerial descent and doctrine to the Apostles than among a new and irregularly formed sect, who set aside the very Scriptures and tradition of the Apostles, boasting that they are correctors of the Apostles.... The heretics have appealed to tradition, answers Irenaeus; then let them be judged by "that tradition which has its origin from the Apostles and has been preserved by a regular succession of presbyters in the Churches"; But when so challenged, "they declare they are wiser than the presbyters, and even than the Apostles," an interesting instance of the authority of private judgement in those days.... There was a tremendous force in the challenge of Tertullian: "Let them show a list of bishops, proceeding in succession from the beginning in such a way that their first bishop had as his authority and predecessor some one of the Apostles or of the apostolic men, who were associated with the Apostles", and in the statement of Irenaeus: "All these (heretics) are of far more recent date than the bishops to whom the Apostles entrusted the Churches."[10]

At this time, Roman law was being introduced and applied to disputes and controversies in the ecclesia, as Ball notes, "Tertullian applies the beneficent principle of the [Roman] law to Catholic doctrine. He claims that beliefs which had held the field from the time of the apostolic Fathers were on that account alone entitled to protection against the new-fangled theories of heretics."[11]

Ignatius went even further by claiming that the bishop stood in the place of the unseen Lord and was thus entrusted with the oversight of the Master's household. Once this conjecture was accepted, it was inevitable that the bishops would come to see that the keys of binding and loosing had been given solely to the *bishops*, as successors of the Apostles—just as in Roman law one governor succeeded another in a province (*ordinatio vicaria*).[12] Those in favor of apostolic succession tenaciously interpreted it that way and, eventually, that interpretation was accepted by all congregations.

But Lindsay dismisses all of this as a "gigantic figment." The most he admits is that apostolic succession "is meant to be a simple and clear

---

10. Hitchcock, 250–51.
11. Ball, 74.
12. Hatch, 106–108.

way to find out what the real faith of the Church is in a time of more than usual perplexity."[13] He emphasizes: "This new theory of the position and authority of the office-bearers in the Christian churches was so novel, and so opposed to the old traditions of primitive Christianity, that an extraordinary sanction was needed to support it, and in the nature of things the sanction had to come down from the earliest days." The concept of apostolic succession was nothing more than a legal fiction created by bishops—most of whom were former lawyers in the Roman State before becoming Christians.[14]

The appeal to and application of Roman law to ecclesiastical doctrine became more widespread as lawyers, like Tertullian, became prominent in the church. Lawyers, by nature, continually seek a legal basis for their decisions, even if they must logically create one to achieve their purpose—a legal fiction. Lindsay explains the use of this legal fiction:

> Apostolic succession, in the dogmatic sense of that ambiguous term, is the legal fiction required by the legal mind to connect the growing conceptions of the authority of the clergy with the earlier days of Christianity. It served the Christian lawyer in much the same way that another curious legal fiction assisted the pagan civilian. The latter insisted that the government of the Emperors from Augustus to Diocletian was the prolongation of the old republican constitution; the former imagined that the rule of bishops was the prolongation through the generations of the inspired guidance of the original apostles who were the planters of the Church. . . . A legal fiction has generally some historical basis to start from. The basis of the fiction in civil law was the fact that the emperors, while wielding almost absolute personal authority, did so in accordance with republican form inasmuch as they were invested by the senate with almost all the offices which under the republic had been distributed among a number of persons. The fiction in ecclesiastical government had also its basis of fact. The apostles had founded many of the churches, and their first converts or others suitable had become the first office-bearers.[15]

Not surprisingly, Cyprian—another former trial lawyer—became the champion of the supremacy of the bishop and laid the groundwork upon which the papacy was eventually erected.

13. Lindsay, 224–25.

14. Ibid., 278.

15. Ibid., 279.

Lightfoot, however, believes the episcopal office was a "providential safeguard amid the confusion of speculative opinion, the distracting effects of persecution, and the growing anarchy of social life, which threatened not only the extension but the very existence of the Church of Christ."[16] He rejects any ulterior motive of power, noting that "ambition of office in a society where prominence of rank involved prominence of risk was at least no vulgar and selfish passion."[17] But, even if the motive was not "vulgar and selfish passion," it may yet have been a claim to power. History is replete with men who have placed themselves at personal risk for power. What is certain is that these newly empowered office-bearers—bishops through apostolic succession—henceforth determined and distinguished correct doctrine from error and heresy. And they spoke with one voice.

With the rescript of Hadrian in 124 CE to Minucius Fundanus, toleration of Christianity became widespread in the Roman Empire.[18] It is during this period that the writings by Christian apologists flourished, requesting accommodation between the imperial government and Christian societies. Converts from all walks flooded into the ecclesiae—wealthy officials, lawyers, merchants, and men and women of culture—and both syncretism and the apathy of everyday life began to infiltrate Christianity. Jesus had declared (Mark 10:22) that possessions and wealth were an obstacle to entrance into the kingdom of God, and this was echoed by James (Jas 2:1–7; 5:1–6) and Paul (1 Tim 6:10). Faced with the shift in social status of those seeking salvation, Clement of Alexandria (c. 150–215 CE) attempted to teach the purpose of wealth by writing *Who Is the Rich Man Who Will Be Saved?* Wealth, though perhaps not intrinsically evil, had but one purpose: charitable works for the sake of the kingdom.

Meanwhile, confronted by the thousands who now sought entrance to the ecclesia, the local ministry began to question just how much of the pagan life or its occupations should be abandoned. If there was to be accommodation on the part of the government, there would also need to be change and accommodation on the part of the Christian societies. The remaining prophets reacted in horror and demanded that believers return to the life of a sojourner—alien residents surrounded, but not compromised, by paganism. Montanism, as we observed, was a reaction not

---

16. Lightfoot, *The Christian Ministry*, 83.
17. Ibid.
18. Lindsay, 229.

only to the restrictions on the prophetic ministry, but to the syncretism that had swept through the congregations.[19]

In time, formal lists of prohibited occupations, like the *Apostolic Tradition*, were modified to accommodate the newly-converted pagans. The bishops began to compromise with the same pagan Roman culture that had once been anathema. Although Tertullian might well argue that a Christian could never be a soldier, his very need to defend his position proves there must have been many who sought a life in the military. A century before, there had never been a need to argue the point.[20] Those in authority "seem to have spontaneously and gradually come to see that it was their duty to bring their followers into what accommodation was possible with the conditions of existing society."[21] Instead of concern for the erosion of what had once constituted holy life, the bishops began to focus more and more on purity of theological doctrine, and the Christian life became something to be protected by creed.

Against the Gnostic and allegorical understanding of Christian teaching, Irenaeus set forth his *fides catholica et apostolica*—a foundation for the understanding of true Christianity. To Irenaeus, this foundation was in less danger of corruption by being in the hands of one man. Truth would be faithfully handed down generation to generation through apostolic succession. One man, in each assembly, became primate—the custodian of the rule of faith.[22]

The very definition of ecclesia changed as well. In its earliest years, the ecclesia had been a brotherhood of saints. It now became a community over whom a bishop presided. It was defined "not so much by the manner of life led by its members as by the government that ruled over them."[23] The train of thought was reversed. The ecclesia was no longer "people worshipping and some of them leading the common devotions, saints believing and some of them instructing and admonishing," but "teachers who impart and pupils who receive, priests who intercede and

---

19. Ibid., 229–33.
20. Ibid., 232.
21. Ibid., 233.
22. Hatch, 96–98.
23. Lindsay, 266.

sinners who are pardoned through intercessions, rulers who command and subjects who are bound to obey."[24]

In addition, the ideal of the universal church underwent an analogous transformation. It became a *visible federation* of local churches, all of whom believed the same verities. It excluded heretics and rebels. Truth was guaranteed by its legitimate rulers, and its members yielded an implicit obedience to the bishop at the head of every local ecclesia.[25]

Norman MacLeod thinks this transformation was providential, but notes that it "must be admitted that from a very early period in the history of Christianity the letter began to prevail over the spirit, and that for many centuries the true idea of the kingdom of Heaven was obscured by the growth of a vast organisation, admirably adapted for the age from which it sprang."[26]

Originally, the authority of the bishop had not extended beyond his own ecclesia, and corporate unity of the ecclesiae was still a sentiment. Ignatius, for example, stated that, as bishop, he was administrator of the finances of his congregation. He might call his congregation together and even administer the sacraments of bread and wine and baptism, but he was not permitted to excommunicate on his own—not even with the approval of the session of elders. His power was limited to moral persuasion.[27]

The notion of the bishop as the *supreme defender of the faith* quickly evolved into the bishop as the *supreme defender of discipline*. This power became especially crucial when dealing with the lapsed and their readmission to the church in the third century, to which we now turn.[28]

During the various and sporadic persecutions that had erupted throughout the empire, but especially during persecution initiated by the emperor Gaius Decius in 250, many Christians recanted their faith to save their lives. These were known as *lapsi* (the lapsed). As Hatch explains, times had changed:

> The sterner discipline had been relaxed. Christianity was not illegal, and was tending to become fashionable. On a sudden the flames of persecution [the Decian persecution] shot fiercely forth

---

24. Ibid.
25. Ibid.
26. MacLeod, 10.
27. Lindsay, 199–200.
28. Hatch, 97–99.

again. The professors of Christian philosophy defended the policy of submission on the theological ground that Christ did not call on all men to be partakers of His sufferings in the flesh. The fashionable church-goers accepted the easy terms which the state offered to those who were willing to acknowledge the state religion. Those who did not actually offer incense on heathen altars made friends with the police, purchased false certificates of having complied with the law, or bribed the officers of the courts to strike their name out of the cause-list. When the persecution was over, many of the "lapsed," as they were called, wished to come back again.[29]

Tertullian had previously determined—by his legalistic and rigorous interpretation of Scripture—that some sins, upon confession, removed a believer for life from full communion with the congregation. Any failure to confess the name of Christ in the face of torture or death was such a sin. Tertullian taught that the penitent lapsed was consigned to be lifelong catechumen. Although that unfortunate soul might attend the congregational meetings, he could never again participate in the Eucharist. He was condemned to wander in the shadowland between salvation and eternal torment for the remainder of his earthly life, as he anxiously awaited God's final determination of his fate at death. It would appear that many had forgotten Peter's denial and restoration—and the lesson of that event.

Those individuals who had suffered for their faith, short of death, and were later released, were known as "martyrs" or "confessors." During the Decian persecution, suffering for the faith became a new beatitude. Since the martyrs had suffered torture for their faith, they were believed to have an intrinsically closer relationship to the Lord, and their prayers were deemed more efficacious. Even those who had suffered the bare minimum were added to their ranks. They were quickly and spontaneously elevated by the congregations to positions of spiritual prominence, were treated with special reverence, and their spiritual counsel was sought on all matters, including readmission to the ecclesia after lapse.

Initially, the bishop and elders in session considered the readmission of the lapsed on a case-by-case basis. The session could be persuaded by the testimony of a confessor on behalf of the lapsed, but, during times of persecution, it was not always convenient for sessions to convene in order to consider the readmission of a lapsed member. In time, this practice

---

29. Ibid., 100–101.

deteriorated to the extent that private pardon by a martyr or confessor entitled the lapsed to restoration of full membership in the community.[30]

Eventually, confessors distributed written certificates of exemption (*libelli*) that entitled its possessor to full restoration of membership in the congregation—without any consent of the elders or bishop—a practice resembling the "indulgences" of the medieval Catholic Church. This state of affairs became a scandal, not only because it fabricated an entirely new and dangerous idea of Christian forgiveness, but because it jeopardized the ecclesiastical control by the bishops, and created a conflict of power between the bishops and the martyr-confessors. The authority of the bishops was in jeopardy.

It would require the firm hand and determination of one bishop from North Africa to settle the issue for all time.

---

30. Ibid., 101–103.

6

The Ecclesia Becomes the Church

Thascius Caecilius Cyprianus (Cyprian) of Carthage was born about 200 CE in North Africa. Before becoming a Christian in 246, Cyprian taught rhetoric and was a successful trial lawyer. After his conversion, he immediately sold his entire estate and devoted himself to sacred studies.[1] Two years later, he was chosen as bishop of Carthage by the acclamation of his entire congregation. "If the filling the vacancy caused by the death of Donatus had been left to the clergy, we would never have heard of him," says John Faulkner.[2] The presbyters thought he was immature and, according to Paul (1 Tim 3:6), ineligible for Church office.

> Cyprian thought so himself and initially declined, wishing an older presbyter to be elected. But the people were inexorable and unanimous. They looked upon him as the strongest and wisest minister in the city, and they would not be refused. They surrounded his house, filled all its approaches, cut off escape, and compelled him to accept.... He was elected by acclamation of the people, which was confirmed by the later assent of all the presbyters except five, and by the ordination of the bishops.[3]

Christians had been persecuted only periodically for the first two hundred years, and most of those persecutions were confined to the larger cities and initiated either at the caprice of the governors or by the enraged populace. As we have seen, Christianity was unlike the existing religions in the Roman Empire, in that it was not polytheistic and it demanded total allegiance within its sphere of influence. From its earliest days, Christianity included a judgment against the existing culture that

---

1. Faulkner, 38.
2. Ibid., 44.
3. Ibid., 44–45.

did not need to be spoken to be understood. It was also unlike Judaism, which had been a *religio licita* (legal religion) since the time of Julius and Augustus. But the Jews did not proselytize. These aspects, coupled with the rigorous limitations on daily life amidst a pagan culture, made Christianity detestable to most people.

Since the death of the emperor Septimius Severus, in February of 211 CE, the church had experienced peace for almost forty years—and had grown spiritually lax. Faulkner remarks that "a time of peace for nation or Church imposes special obligations of watchfulness and discipline and self-denial, lest corruptions creep in and the inheritance be lost. And in a Catholic Church these corruptions are almost inevitable. . . . That God will not prevent by extraordinary means what may be avoided by the simple paths of His Gospel, history is a witness."[4]

As bishop of Carthage, Cyprian immediately set to work restoring church discipline. The church had always condemned the profession of acting and had denied baptism to actors or anyone who frequented the theater. In one case presented to Cyprian for judgment, a former actor had been earning his living by teaching the profession to boys, to make up for his lost income. Cyprian condemned this as outright hypocrisy. Faulkner relates the story:

> [Cyprian] refers to the "disgraceful and infamous practices of the theater, emasculation of boys and men, men putting on women's garments, immodest gestures, and the gratification of the desire by the sins of a corrupted and enervated body." If it is a sin for one to act in the theater, is it not to teach others the same? If he is compelled to this by poverty, let the Church support him frugally, and if the Church is not able, let him come to us. Such was the advice of Cyprian. The Church denied baptism and communion to frequenters of the theater, not to speak of actors, and she did wisely in this, because the theater was not only connected with idolatry, but was an inciter and purveyor to sin and vice in various and influential ways,—it was then and ever has remained the foremost opponent to all the ideals for which the Church stands.[5]

As it turned out, the theater finally proved too great an adversary for the church, and its bishops were forced to relent on the issue. Eventually,

---

4. Ibid., 47–48.
5. Ibid., 51–52.

the bishops had to content themselves with mere denunciations and warnings.⁶

Cyprian also assailed women who had taken up the same manner of adornment as the society around them. "Has God willed that holes should be made in the ears, by which the children should be put to pain, so that subsequently heavy beads should be hung? Such arts as the sinning and apostate angels put forth. It was they who taught women to pain [sic] the eyes around with a black circle, to stain the cheeks with a deceitful red, to change the hair, and drive out truth both of face and head."⁷

During the intervening years of peace, many bishops had focused on moneymaking, at the expense of their responsibilities to the congregations. They had become slave traders, merchants and investors, landlords, shop owners, makers of idols, and compounders of incense.⁸ Cyprian attacked this syncretism that had crept into the church. He describes his fellow bishops: "They with insatiable ardor of covetousness devoted themselves to the increase of their property. . . . [The bishops] despised the divine charge, became agents in business, deserted their people, wandered about in foreign provinces, hunted the markets for gainful merchandise, while brethren were starving in the Church. They sought to possess money in hoards, they seized estates by crafty deceits, they increased their gains by multiplying usuries."⁹ His remedy was "discipline, discipline the safeguard of hope, the bond of faith, the guide of the way of salvation, the stimulus and nourishment of good dispositions, the teacher of virtue, which causes us to abide always in Christ, and to live continually for God, and to attain the heavenly promises and the divine rewards."¹⁰

Such was the state of the church as Cyprian found it prior to the great Decian persecution. He became bishop probably in July, 248 CE, and the Decian persecution began at the end of 249 or the beginning of 250. Faulkner provides important historic background to this major persecution.

> It must be remembered that until Decius there were no express laws against the Christians as such. Their trials proceeded always

6. Ibid., 52.
7. Ibid., 54.
8. Faulkner, 55–56.
9. Ibid., 49.
10. Ibid., 56.

under the general police or criminal jurisprudence of the empire; which was not closely defined or limited, but was general and elastic, and left large play to the individual judgment or caprice of the president of the court who was the prefect, proconsul, or governor. The civil law of Rome was fixed fast, with well understood rules; the criminal law was not. It was something like the police power of a modern State, which can soon override the people's liberties in case of assumed necessity, like an uproar, mutiny, riot, etc., or like the power of a ship captain. For this reason a tolerant and free thinking governor, or even a careless and Gallio-like one, could let the Christians go if he thought there were no immediate danger to the State; while an upright and strict ruler, patriotic and devoted to the national ideals, could easily set the forces of persecution at work.[11]

Cults that were confined to the Roman provinces were given the opportunity of becoming a *religio licita* by registration with the authorities, but since Christianity was not confined to a province, it could not be registered.[12] As Edward White Benson explains, it was

a *tertium genus*, not ethnic, nor Judaic; and any other associations for religious rites, save only unions for securing funeral celebrations for their members, were illicit. It is strange to think that the Church must have subsisted for some time at Rome under the external aspect of a Burial Society; occupied its catacombs, had its staff of fossors [grave diggers], and entombed its martyrs in this light. No clubs except those of very poor persons were allowed to have common funds; they might not assemble oftener than once a month; and no permanent "Master of sacred rites" [*magister sacrorum*] was allowed. The State was the one society which should engross every religious and social interest beyond those of the family. Monotheism even when licensed was looked on as anti-national and anti-imperial.[13]

Christians were suspect in the eyes of the Roman magistrate because they were a monotheistic society,[14] they came from all classes, and their secret societies existed throughout the empire; they met daily and de-

11. Faulkner, 61.
12. Benson, 61.
13. Ibid., 61.
14. Jews were monotheistic, but they did not try to make proselytes; and their cultic center was demolished in 70 AD. Faulkner, 61.

ferred to their religious superiors. Since informers (*delatores*) were everywhere and richly rewarded, Christians were constantly in danger of being charged with treason (*leges maiestatis*).[15]

The initial response by the magistrate to suspicious or treasonous acts was the application of a test, which took two forms.

> While a slave or provincial could be tortured, a freeman, suspect of religious engagements hostile to the State, could be summoned to take part in a sacrificial feast, or at least to offer incense before an imperial statue, to which the least mark of disrespect was treason. Whatever other scruples were allowed for, none might doubt the present divinity of the emperor; no beliefs could interfere with a mechanical act of obedient veneration.[16]

Under the *Rex Legia*, all imperial edicts required the application of a test.[17] It was competent for

> any magistrate, who suspected or feared the growth of a dangerous class in his district, or was pressed by popular feeling, to summon a neighbourhood or any residents in it to take the test under former edicts. This mode of action is exhibited in far the larger number of arrests which led to confessorship and martyrdom. "Persecution" of this kind, as the Christians very naturally called it, was incessantly simmering in some province or other, intensified by the policy of one emperor, moderated by the broader policy of another, at times ceasing for years in particular districts.[18]

Repeated torture was commonly applied to slaves and provincials as an incentive to confess the suspected crime.[19] But, in the case of Christians, it was applied because, as Benson notes, "to be a Christian was equivalent to having gross crimes to confess. A secret society which could not ask

---

15. Benson, 61–62.
16. Ibid., 62.
17. Ibid.
18. Ibid. Benson also notes: "To quit the army prematurely without approved cause was treason. For a Christian to remain unsuspected or if suspected to avoid disobedience was scarcely possible. The sacrifices to the standards, the military oaths, the religious decorations, the festivities, the wreaths distributed not simply in honour of the emperor but in honour of his divinity, were endless snares. Thus the martyrologies name many soldiers. And if the victims of a town persecution were easily multiplied by report, the deaths of disloyal privates in a regiment would seldom transpire." Benson, 62–63.
19. Paul was very nearly subjected to the test in Jerusalem (Acts 22:25–29).

for a license, which at Rome pretended to be a burial society, and was evidently much more, lay under charges of hideous unnatural orgies."[20]

In all cases where it was applied, torture was repeated several times, in order to preclude the possibility that the admission was only obtained through pain. After repeated and consistent confession, the accused was then tortured to make him deny Christ, since it was common knowledge that denial would automatically exclude him from the Christian sect. Thus, by achieving denial of Christ, the magistrate felt certain he had obtained what amounted to a promise to be guilty no more.[21]

As we observed in Pliny's letter to Trajan, the magistrate often considered his actions benevolent—a characteristic that Benson notes of *genuine* martyrdom accounts.[22] The Roman magistrate considered torture to be a lenient discipline. "He could not understand their declining to be let off so cheaply. He did not consider it a punishment at all, but a condonation of the past while it sufficiently secured the State from a repetition of the offences. The secret crimes whatever they might be were allowed to pass in the account."[23]

Thus, the Decian persecution sought primarily the *apostasy* and not the death of Christian adherents.

> The result was that torture was applied everywhere with unrelenting rigor and persistence. This fact accounts for many recantations. It is much easier to meet death at once, than it is to endure days of excruciating pain. The Christians were thrown into prison, loaded with chains, and their limbs stretched on the rack; their fingers were crushed, their joints dislocated, and their flesh torn with nails and hooks. Sometimes the victims were exposed to extreme heat, and left for days in the torture of thirst. They were burnt with charcoal and red-hot irons. Some were stripped, smeared with honey, and exposed to the sting of insects. Everywhere the Christians

---

20. Benson, 63.
21. Ibid.
22. Ibid.

23. Ibid., 63. Benson adds that, eventually, attempts to repress the superstition of Christianity became more fruitless and desperate. In the minds of the Roman authorities, there existed a real danger that the entire system of public worship and domestic religion, which supported what he calls the "sobriety of morals among a large class of the population," would be disturbed "before the undisguised contempt of men who acknowledged none of the authorised sanctions and were believed to live in private shamelessness." Benson, 64.

were insulted, stoned, beaten, robbed of their possessions, and, in case they were constant to their faith, put to death.[24]

Decius was relentless in his attack on what had become a universal and organized institution in the intervening years.[25] In his mind, it was all the more dangerous to the empire because it was an institution. His first strategy was to decapitate the organization by executing the bishops, believing that the body would die as a consequence. Many were executed, while many others saved their lives through flight. Though Cyprian was initially reluctant to do so, his congregation insisted that he flee as well.

Thousands of ordinary believers were dragged before tribunals and either lost their lives or were jailed, tortured, or banished. But the Decian persecution was hardly universal. Many parts of the empire saw no persecution at all, or endured only a brief one. After that persecution faded, the congregations again faced the problem of the lapsed. Many bishops thought the idea of pardon through the application to a martyr was too similar to the power the prophetic ministry had once enjoyed. It was this presumption by the martyrs and confessors—that they possessed power at least equal to the bishop—which Callistus, bishop of Rome (218–222 CE), immediately recognized as a danger to established order. Cyprian would face the problem as well.[26]

Faulkner describes the events while Cyprian was still in hiding. "Four presbyters wrote to Cyprian in the first stage of the persecution (between February and April, 250) to move him to show mildness to the lapsed, and to give peace to the dying. Cyprian did not comply. Soon after came the second stage of the persecution when there was a possibility to help the [lapsed] by the martyrs."[27] Some of the presbyters took advantage of Cyprian's silence and, on their own initiative, granted communion to the lapsed who possessed a martyr's certificate—without waiting for the decision of the bishop. Upon his return, Cyprian immediately reclaimed

---

24. Moxom, 205.

25. One example will illustrate how institutionalized the church had become. Fabian, bishop of Rome (236–250 CE), assigned two of the fourteen regions of Rome to each of his seven deacons. "To each of the deacons there was a subdeacon and six acolytes. Exorcists, readers and doorwatchers amounted to fifty-two. Such was the administrative body required for the fifty thousands Christians of Rome in the middle of the third century." Benson, 67–68.

26. Faulkner, 86.

27. Faulkner, 88–89.

what he considered an important power—a power that Cyprian insisted resided only in the bishop.

Cyprian was eventually successful in his struggle against the right of the martyrs and confessors to pronounce pardon. The Synods of Carthage in 251 and 252 CE established the complete supremacy of the local office-bearers over the martyrs—and it was never again questioned.[28]

Cyprian precipitated an evolution in the office of the bishop. He theorized that the bishop was the representative (*antistes*) of Christ in his congregation.[29] But his conception of the bishop did not include the primacy of Rome or any other church.[30] In spite of this, ultimately, Cyprian's autocratic bishop was indeed transformed into the idea of *Pontifex Maximus*—as Tertullian had so presciently and sarcastically called what ultimately became the papacy.[31]

Long before Cyprian, the Eucharist and the Agape had become emphatically differentiated.[32] The *Canons of Hippolytus*[33] describes the Agape as obviously private and under the direction of the bishop. But superstition had also crept into the entire ceremony—special care must be taken, the sacred elements must be guarded, and no crumb must be dropped, lest an evil spirit get hold of it.[34] By the second century, the historic and traditional communal banquet had become too disorderly and inappropriate in the minds of the bishops. For a time, the Agape continued to be celebrated apart from the Eucharist in private homes; but, since it required the presence of the bishop, it was ultimately abandoned. The Council of Laodicea (c. 363 CE) finally directed that it was "not lawful to hold the so-called Agapae in the Churches, or assemblies, and to eat, or set out couches in the house of God."[35]

Cyprian also introduced the novel theory that the Eucharist was a sacrifice and that a special priesthood stood in the place of God on earth.

28. Lindsay, 298.
29. Ibid., 305.
30. Ibid., 318.
31. Ibid., 335.
32. Keating, 100, 104.
33. Lindsay says the *Canons of Hippolytus* "contains the clearest description of Christian public worship which we have between the Epistle of St. Paul to the Corinthians and the much later *Apostolic Constitutions*." For his analysis, see Lindsay, 245–58.
34. Canon 29; Lindsay, 258.
35. Canon 28; Keating, 151–52.

He conceived the bishop's role as that of a priest. "The priest may be defined as one who represents God to man and man to God."[36] In Cyprian's mind, the Eucharist was a sacrifice offered by a priest—the bishop.[37] In similar fashion, Clement had previously adduced, from the Aaronic priesthood and Temple service, "that God had appointed set persons and set places, and will have all things done in order."[38] Benson comments on this idea:

> The Jewish Priesthood at last became "a name and a shade," on the day when it crucified Christ. Its reality passed on to the Christian bishop; each congregation (diocese) is "the congregation of Israel"; the election of the bishop in their presence is made in accordance with the Law of Moses; the lapsed or sinful bishop is prohibited from sacrificing by the Mosaic statute against uncleanness; his communicants are tainted by his sin. The presbyterate is the Levitic tribe: exempt from worldly office, debarred from worldly callings, living on the offerings of the people, as their predecessors on the tithes, devoted day and night to sacrifice and prayer. So precise is the application, that the people are to rise at their coming in pursuance of the Levitic direction.
>
> Again there is another aspect of the same office. The Apostles were bishops. Matthias was ordained a "bishop." And still the bishop is the Apostle of his flock. From the Twelve through successive ordinations he derives that character. His order is of divine creation. The diaconate is the institution of his predecessors.
>
> He is not only a Judge. He is Judge in Christ's stead. Contempt of his government is the parent of heresy; it is expressly condemned in the Law, in the books of Samuel, by the example of St Paul and of our Lord. To maintain the same faith and worship and yet invade the office of the rightful bishop is identically the sin of Korah. For the Laws about the High Priest are not merely applicable to the Bishops; they were ultimately intended for them, and now they apply to them alone. . . . What is distinctive therefore in Cyprian's theory simply regards the origin of that office. According to him, it is (1) an inheritance from the apostles, (2) and a succession to the Levitic Priesthood, only more glorious in being the fulfilment of that priest-

---

36. Lightfoot, *The Christian Ministry*, 132.
37. Lindsay, 309.
38. Lightfoot, *The Christian Ministry*, 106.

hood as of a type. . . . From the very first Cyprian believed that he read that doctrine in Scripture, and in Scripture as a whole.[39]

Tertullian had also held a sacerdotal view of the ministry, although in a rudimentary form.[40] The analogy of the sacrifices and the correspondence of the threefold order (bishops, presbyters, and deacons) supplied the needed material upon which this sacerdotal feeling operated.[41] But this nice, legal fiction does not prove that the clergy has its origin in the Jewish priesthood.[42]

As MacLeod states,

> No Ministry can relieve the individual soul of its responsibility or rob it of its privilege of personal and immediate approach unto God. The Gospel interposes no sacerdotal system or priestly caste between the Father of our spirits and His children. When the Holy Ghost is setting forth the office of Christian Ministers they are spoken of under various titles. They are called *Shepherds, Watchmen, Stewards, Servants, Ambassadors*. But not in one single instance are they called priests.[43]

By the middle of the third century, the Christian church began modeling itself on the organization of the imperial cult.[44] Benson disputes that this was the case. "I see no proof, and to me it is incredible, that [Cyprian or others] . . . should have derived any such scheme, consciously or unconsciously, from Pagan constitutions, which appeared to them all in the light of a purely demoniacal and satanic system."[45] Obviously, the bishops and laity viewed paganism as satanic; but, as Lindsay points out, "The vestments of the clergy, unknown in [the] early centuries—dalmatic, chasuble, stole and maniple—were all taken over by the Christian clergy from the Roman magistracy; the word *Bull*, to denote a papal rescript, was borrowed from the old imperial administration."[46] The church in Rome created various lower orders of readers, exorcists, doorkeepers,

---

39. Benson, 33–34, 39.
40. Lightfoot, *The Christian Ministry*, 115–16.
41. Ibid., 128.
42. Ibid., 105.
43. MacLeod, 34.
44. Hatch, 164; Lindsay, 353–55.
45. Benson, 40.
46. Lindsay, 353.

gravediggers. Acolytes and doorkeepers were imitations of the officials in the state temples.[47] Celsus noted, as late as 170 CE, that the Christians had no altars. But by 200, the table where the Eucharist was offered was called "the altar."[48]

It might be argued that the first-century ecclesiae had previously incorporated selective organizational elements of the surrounding pagan institutions, and that the adoption of elements from the imperial cult was nothing more than an extension of that idea; but the ecclesiae had adapted certain elements of the social organizations of Roman society, without adopting their religious elements and trappings. In contrast, those elements incorporated by the church from the imperial cult were its pagan *religious* trappings. What is significant is that the bishops were not offended by the introduction of these cultic elements into the church. In their minds, the church might adopt anything from paganism and Christianize it.

But it was Cyprian's intrusion into the controversy over the election of Novatian that firmly and conclusively established the power of the bishop. During the controversy over lapsed members, the Roman faithful had divided into two parties. The puritan party held to a rigorous position that the lapsed could never be restored to full fellowship. The anti-puritan party held that the ecclesia contained both the weak and the strong, the clean and unclean, as had Noah's ark, and that the lapsed could be restored upon repentance.[49] The seat of the Roman bishop had been vacant for some time when Cornelius was finally elected to that office (251 CE). He belonged to the anti-puritan party. In response, the puritan party legally elected Novatian—its nominal head—as their bishop. Both parties claimed the legal right to establish independent congregations.

Cyprian believed that the office of bishop represented both unity of doctrine and unity of discipline, and settled the conflict. He declared that, since Rome was organized as a single body, there could be but one bishop. He wrote to Cornelius: "The seamless coat of Christ must not be rent."[50] Just as there is one God, one Christ, and one Holy Spirit, so could there

---

47. Ibid., 354.
48. Arnold, *The Early Christians*, 33; Lindsay, 257.
49. Hatch, 102.
50. Ibid., 105.

be only one bishop in each city. Novatian was deposed.[51] The necessity for unity outweighed all other considerations. As a further consequence of Cyprian's decision, anyone claiming membership in the Christian Church was forced to become a member of the one established congregation in that city.[52] In 829, the Council of Paris established a more complete doctrine based on Cyprian's interpretation.[53]

Cyprian's theory that the bishop was the representative of Christ, coupled with the new sacerdotal character of the office, provided the foundation for even further expansion of the bishop's authority—namely, that the gifts bestowed at baptism through the laying on of hands were bestowed solely by the hands of the bishop. What had formerly been the function of a session of elders was now expropriated by the bishop alone. Little by little, those members of the Christian congregations who did not hold an office were excluded from the performance of almost all ecclesiastical functions.[54] The *Canons of Hippolytus* preserved that structure that still exists—the two great divisions of rank and function within the church—the *plebs* (laity) and the *ordo* (pastors, elders, deacons, and bishop). Both terms were drawn from Roman law.[55]

Montanism had failed in its attempt to arrest the increasing dominance of the local ministry. That failure had only solidified the power of the bishops. "The tendency was to think that the churches were summed up in their bishops, and these officials thus acquired a new position with reference to the whole Church."[56] But other forces were also at work in establishing the supremacy of the office-bearers.

For decades, the church had argued that it was entitled to the toleration extended to all other religions. In order to facilitate toleration, it attempted to come to some accommodation with the world lying round the Christian communities. The bishops recognized that the new converts—those who had flocked to it during periods of peace—would fall away if they insisted upon the former, higher standards of Christian conduct. They feared the new converts would return to heathenism. The practical

---

51. Ibid.
52. Ibid.
53. Ibid., 108–109.
54. Ibid., 127.
55. Lindsay, 245 n 2.
56. Ibid., 273.

consequence of these ideas was a revision of the thought and conditions of penitence.

The status of the lapsed still loomed. In earlier times, when a Christian fell into grievous sins, such as idolatry, murder, adultery, fornication and others, the unfortunate soul could never be received again into full communion, but had to remain a catechumen—"permitted to wait in the ante-chamber but never admitted within the family abode until death was at hand."[57] But, if the church is the indispensable means of salvation, so that apart from her no one can be saved—Cyprian's position—then it is cruel to deny readmission. Thus, Cyprian's doctrine of the church inevitably led to generous dealings with all sinners.[58]

Callistus, bishop of Rome, had been the first to assert that the power of the church was exercised through its office-bearers. By means of this innovation, he reasoned the bishops were entitled to proclaim God's pardon for any sin, however heinous. He declared that the church in Rome would permit a second trial of the full Christian life—but a second fall was not to be forgiven.[59]

Tertullian and Hippolytus vehemently opposed this change in doctrine,[60] and some North African churches kept to the old practice up to the time of Cyprian. But the Roman example was largely followed.[61] Probably from the very beginning, "the Church of Rome exhibited that strongly marked legal and disciplinarian character which it has borne ever since.... It is not surprising that in Rome, the centre of the Empire and the very fountain of law and order, religion should have seized the reins of authority more decisively than elsewhere."[62]

THE IMPERIAL CHURCH

About five months after his conquest of Italy (313 CE), Constantine, and his co-regent Licinius, published the Edict of Milan, which was received as law

---

57. Ibid., 273–74.
58. Faulkner, 118.
59. Lindsay, 274.
60. Ibid.
61. Ibid., 275.
62. Bigg, 22.

in the Roman world.⁶³ That edict terminated the persecution of Christianity and permitted freedom of religion to all. Gibbon notes that it

> provided for the restitution of all the civil and religious rights of which the Christians had been so unjustly deprived. It was enacted that the places of worship, and public lands, which had been confiscated, should be restored to the church, without dispute, without delay, and without expense: and this severe injunction was accompanied with a gracious promise that, if any of the purchasers had paid a fair and adequate price, they should be indemnified from the Imperial treasury.⁶⁴

According to Schaff, "This was the first proclamation of the great principle that every man had a right to choose his religion according to the dictates of his own conscience and honest conviction, without compulsion and interference from the government. Religion is worth nothing except as an act of freedom. A forced religion is no religion at all."⁶⁵ But Schaff somewhat romantically overstates this turn of events; ultimately, the bishops were not satisfied with mere legal equality.

Nonetheless, Christianity stepped confidently toward the throne, under the shadow and protection of its favorite and champion, Constantine—falsely regarded as the first Christian emperor. Constantine, for his part, was content to dissemble. In his mind, Christianity was simply one of many ways to approach the deity. He directed the continuation of the pagan haruspices.⁶⁶ The sun, in the form of Apollo, was his invincible and constant guide, and he even styled the Lord's Day as *dies solis* (Sunday), so as not to offend pagan ears.⁶⁷ He was baptized a Christian catechumen only hours before his death on May 22, 337 CE. As he had ordered, his body was pretentiously interred amongst twelve empty sarcophagi, representing the twelve apostles.

It is pure folly to excuse, justify, or minimize Constantine's many bloody crimes by claiming that his actions must be understood within the context of that age, or because "he took a sincere interest in the progress of the Christian cause, and laboured to the best of his knowledge and

---

63. Gibbon, 1:291.
64. Gibbon, 1:291.
65. Schaff, *History of the Christian Church*, 2:72–73.
66. Gibbon, 1:290.
67. Ibid., 1:759 n 8.

ability for the peace and unity of the Church."[68] His supposed vision of the labarum, prior to the battle at the Milvian Bridge, made the sword an immutable part of the cross. Together with the fawning bishops who groveled at his feet, Constantine bequeathed to succeeding generations his confused perversion of Christianity—a grotesque farrago.

After recognition by the state, and in keeping with its new imperial status, it was clearly advisable that the church should be homogenous.[69] Councils flourished throughout the empire and continued in their efforts to precisely define orthodoxy. Under the guidance of its presumed Christian prince, the church officially recognized excommunication as universal, instead of locally enforced, as it had been. In 314 CE, the Council of Arles determined "[soldiers] who throw down their arms in time of peace shall be excommunicate."[70]

The power of excommunication ensured compliance with civil law and provided a very real deterrent to objection or schism—and it had the force of the magistrate to support it.[71] Later edicts declared that no one could join another Christian congregation in the empire without having in hand a certificate of good standing from his former bishop. Absence of a certificate not only cut the individual off from ecclesiastical and eternal security, but social intercourse and employment as well. Commingled with the power of the state, "the Christian Churches passed from their original state of independence into a great confederation."[72]

Toleration of all religions as equals was not long sustained. In 391 CE, Emperor Theodosius outlawed all pagan sacrifices and declared Christianity the only true religion. By the end of the fourth century, Christianity was the dominant political and social force in the empire.[73] It became the religion of the state, and heresy became a political crime and was eradicated by imperial fiat.[74] The basilicas and private property of heretics were confiscated. Heretics were barred from assembly, were prohibited from bequeathing or inheritance, were banished, were excluded

68. Orr, 150; Duchesne, 2:71.
69. Hatch, 172.
70. Canon 3; Deissmann, 210.
71. Hatch, 175–78.
72. Ibid., 175, 182.
73. Ibid., 144.
74. Ibid.

from civil service, and were liable to fines. Heretical writings were hunted and burned, and the concealing of any banned books became a capital offense.[75]

The once broad border between the church and the world became less defined as a consequence of the recognition of the church by the state. The fact that judges and emperors were now "Christian" diminished the need for submitting disputes to the church officers. The natural effect was that Christians presented their cases in court.[76]

Incredibly, in spite of the ascendency of a monolithic episcopate, the early types of ecclesiastical organization still survived at the beginning of the fourth century in some of the more remote areas of the empire. But, by the end of that century, the early forms had almost completely disappeared, largely as a result of the establishment of a separate class of religious officials—the clergy.

The word *clergy* is derived from the word "lot" (κλῆρον)—the lot, by which an office is assigned and the body of persons holding that office.[77] According to Hatch, the causes that produced a separate clergy class were (1) the state conceding to the officers of the Christian churches those immunities that had been enjoyed previously by the heathen priesthood and by some of the liberal professions, and (2) the state granting to the officers of the Christian churches an exemption from the ordinary jurisdiction of the civil courts—that is, the clergy were beyond the reach of the magistrate. The joint effect of the exemptions from public burdens and from ordinary courts was the creation of a class that was civilly distinct from the rest of the community.[78]

Lindsay points out that the idea of the clergy as a separate class had been checked in early years by the prohibition of a stipend from the congregation.[79] Pastors, elders, and deacons had received money from the common treasury only if impoverished.[80] In keeping with Paul's admonition to the Ephesian elders at Miletus (Acts 20:34–35), most bishops—indeed the entire local ministry—held a trade during the first two centuries.

---

75. Ibid., 181n.
76. Ibid., 75.
77. Lightfoot, 103.
78. Hatch, 146–50, 154.
79. Lindsay, 203–204; Hatch, 154.
80. Ibid., 202–203.

This earlier understanding of Paul's admonition was conveniently redefined when the Edict of Toleration permitted the congregations to hold property. Ironically, the Montanists had been the first to propose the idea of a paid pastorate in the second century. Their idea had been roundly condemned as heretical and alien to Catholic practice.[81]

Eight years after the Edict of Milan, Constantine granted to all his subjects the free and universal permission of bequeathing their fortunes to the holy Catholic Church.[82] He enrolled widows and orphans in the public allowance, and, in some cases, gave the churches the revenue of heathen temples. As a result, the clergy and the bishops became a moneyed class.[83] In time, they became so wealthy that they lent at interest—even though this had been forbidden by provincial councils.[84]

But this was not a novel development. The bishops had spiritually run aground a century and a half earlier, as John Kaye notes:

> After Tertullian's secession from the Church, his respect for the episcopal office, or rather perhaps for the individuals who were in his day appointed to it, appears to have undergone a considerable diminution. He insinuates that they were actuated by worldly motives; and ascribes to their anxiety to retain their power and emoluments a practice, which had been introduced into some Churches, of levying contributions upon the members, for the purpose of bribing the governors and military to connive at the religious meetings of the Christians.[85]

Selwyn comments on this deterioration: "And yet the attempt at conciliation of two incompatible things, the fellowship of Christ and indulgence in sensual lust, would continue to be made, and the Gospel must pass through that phase of its existence in which it is well-nigh choked with the riches and pleasures of this life."[86] In the words of Robert Ingersoll: "The Church has always been willing to swap off treasures in heaven for cash down."

As the church adjusted to its new status, comfort, and security, the struggle for moral purity was converted into a struggle against human

---

81. Beaty, 111.
82. Gibbon, 1:301.
83. Hatch, 154–55.
84. Ibid., 154.
85. Kaye, 226–27.
86. Selwyn, *St. Luke the Prophet*, 260.

nature itself.[87] As asceticism and separation from society became virtues to be pursued, monastic communities sprang up. Just as Montanism had been a reaction to the dissolution of the prophetic ministry, so monasticism was a reaction to the comfort, security, and syncretism of the church. At first, it existed only on the fringe of Christianity. But, when persecution ceased, the monastic life became a choice for those who wished to mortify the flesh voluntarily. It was also during this period that the bishops and clergy embraced celibacy as an enforced virtue.

Eventually, the clergy were barred from ordinary pursuits and amusements. "They had a separate civil status, they had separate emoluments, they were subject to special rules of life. The shepherd bishop driving his cattle to their rude pasturage among the Cyprian hills, the merchant bishop of North Africa, the physician presbyter of Rome, were vanished types whose living examples could be found no more."[88] Hatch adds, "To the [pagans] of Gaul and Spain, to the Celtic inhabitants of [Britain], and, in rather later times, to the Teutonic races of Central Europe, [the clergy] were probably never known except as a special class, assuming a special status, living a special life, and invested with special powers."[89]

When the bishops and clergy ascended the throne as co-regents with their champion emperors, thousands more, who would never have sought fellowship with Christ, poured into the church. Rather than teach the hollow shell of what had once been the doctrine and life of the early believers, it permitted these pagans to bring with them all sorts of abominable trappings and practices from their heathen religions. Mariolatry, feasts and fasts, Lenten vows, lauds and vespers, shrines, and the worship of saints and relics all become established during this period, and were merely the accommodation and incorporation of various pagan elements by church. Not only did the church permit and accept these adulterations, it blessed them, hallowed them—all in the mistaken belief that whatever the church blesses may be used in service to Christ.

When Christianity became the state religion of the Roman Empire, the expression *extra ecclesiam nulla salus*[90]—a warning first used against paganism—was turned against those Christians who would not accept

---

87. Hatch, 156.
88. Ibid., 163.
89. Ibid., 164.
90. "Outside (or, apart from) the church there is no salvation."

the orthodoxy of the bishops and clergy. The church had long since protected itself against any protestations from the prophetic ministry or any other group. The prophetic ministry had been eclipsed and the martyrs had been checked in their attempt to grasp authority. The local ministry, under the direction of the bishop, had no superiors to interfere with them or to supersede them in exhortation, in the dispensing of the Holy Supper, and in prescribing how Christians ought to live in the fear of God.[91] From the fourth century, Christianity eradicated all opposing doctrine by either excommunication or the sword.

> Safe within the fold of the State, [Christians] could speak of themselves as the one Catholic Church of Christ outside of which there was no salvation; they could apply to their own circle of churches all the metaphors and promises of Old Testament prophecy and all the sublime descriptions of the Epistle to the Ephesians, while their fellow-Christians who were outside state protection were being exterminated.[92]

The church had rejected the prophetic ministry, had erected its own authority, had acquiesced on doctrine and life, and had joined itself to the state. To its own detriment and at the cost of its spirit and inheritance, the ecclesia had become the institutional church.

---

91. Lindsay, 244.
92. Ibid., 361.

7

Excursus on the Episcopacy

THIS CHAPTER AND THE next examine (1) the arguments supporting the episcopacy and (2) the cessation of the miraculous, or supernatural, gifts in the ecclesia. But, as these two chapters may seem to be appended or out of place, a brief explanation is in order. Though not logically necessary, these two discussions have value, because knowing how "things have moved better enables us to understand the logical process whereby they tend towards a particular goal in the future."[1] To have included these discussions earlier in the text would have forced too great a diversion of thought. They are best examined separately and after the historical events surrounding them have been surveyed.

Now, it is clear that the episcopacy was the general trend of church government after the prophetic ministry was eclipsed, and before the papacy—its logical outgrowth—appeared. The episcopacy is so significant that Gibbon devotes a considerable portion of his fifteenth chapter to it. In light of its historical prominence and importance, we need to examine the arguments purporting to establish it. The argument for the cessation of the miraculous gifts is no less important, since both issues are bound together—for, in order for the episcopacy to be valid, it is *essential* that the miraculous or supernatural gifts are no longer present in the church.

Apostolic succession implies that Jesus gave the apostles at least the authority to ordain legitimate successors to their functions in the ecclesiae. Moreover, if the episcopacy, through apostolic succession, is actually what Jesus intended to be the rule of government in the ecclesiae, all other forms of ecclesiastical organization are in error.

What is the evidence to support apostolic succession and the episcopacy?

1. Belloc, 28.

The idea of the episcopacy appears suddenly in the subapostolic writings, shortly before the second century. Its development is not recorded. With the singular exception of the reactionary movement of Montanism, we find none of the debate that occurs over doctrine. It simply appears—an accomplished fact. Attempts to prove its legitimacy are scant. Clement is the first, in 96 CE, and later Irenaeus, as we noted in chapter 5. Most congregations slowly embrace it, but not all.

Lightfoot writes:

> As late therefore as the year 70 no distinct signs of episcopal government have hitherto appeared in Gentile Christendom. Yet unless we have recourse to a sweeping condemnation of received documents, it seems vain to deny that early in the second century the episcopal office was firmly and widely established. Thus during the last three decades of the first century, and consequently during the lifetime of the latest surviving Apostle, this change must have been brought about. But the circumstances under which it was effected are shrouded in darkness; and various attempts have been made to read the obscure enigma.[2]

When the episcopacy appeared, new limitations were placed on the prophetic ministry. These restrictions eventually increased until prophecy, as an abiding gift in the ecclesiae, was reduced to a mere ideal. No one was bold enough to claim that the prophetic ministry had disappeared completely, but no bishop wept over its scarcity.

The role of the bishop also changed during this period, as Lowrie notes: "The pastoral and teaching functions fell more and more into the hands of the bishop as the charismatic ministry became rarer. But the

---

2. Lightfoot, *The Christian Ministry*, 31. Lightfoot and many others assume that John lived almost to the close of the first century because of a misunderstanding of historic events. The belief that John was condemned to the isle of Patmos during the reign of Domitian (81–96 CE) is based upon the earliest extant statement by Victorinus (martyred 303 CE) in his commentary on Revelation: "When John saw these things, he was in the isle of Patmos, condemned to the mines by Domitian Caesar." This statement has always forced the date of Revelation to sometime after 81. What historians *continue* to ignore is that Domitian was invested with *full consular authority* for six months in 70, as his father Vespasian sped back to Rome from Egypt to take the crown. Dion Cassius relates that Vespasian wrote to Domitian during the journey: "I am much obliged to you, my son, for letting me still be emperor, and for not having as yet deposed me" (*Rom. Hist.* 65. 22.66.1–3). In fact, John may have been banished to Patmos by Domitian during those six months. He may have died well before 80 CE and never lived to see these changes in church polity. For a complete discussion, see Edmundson, 166–79 and Robinson, 221–53.

fact that such functions fell to him at all, must remain a riddle so long as we suppose that his office was originally in its functions antipodal to the teaching office."[3]

For those who defend the episcopacy, like Gore, these rapid developments are both expected and normal. Gore is the most prominent champion of the episcopacy and apostolic succession. He is adamant that the episcopacy was providentially ordained and that it is the only true form of ecclesiastical government. He begins by asking if Jesus ever specified how the Christian congregations were to be organized.

> The question is whether believers in Christ were left to organize themselves in societies by the natural attraction of sympathy in beliefs and aims, and are, therefore, still at liberty to organize themselves on any model which seems from time to time to promise the best results, or whether the divine Founder of the Christian religion Himself instituted a society, a brotherhood, to be the home of the grace and truth which He came to bring to men: so that becoming His disciple, meant from the first this—in a real sense this only—incorporation into His society.[4]

He continues his argument by laying out three premises:

> It must be admitted that if the documents of the New Testament stood alone—if Christianity had vanished from the world and these documents had been disinterred and constituted our sole evidence of the nature of an ancient religion—we should feel that various tendencies towards different kinds of organization were at work in the Christian church, that the picture presented was confused, and that no decisive conclusion as to the form of the Christian ministry could be reached. But in fact the documents of the New Testament are only some of the documents which belong to a great historical movement. And the tendency of the whole movement—the disentangling of tendencies and the emergence of dominant principles—guides us in attributing more or less importance to this or that phenomenon. The earliest history must be interpreted in the light of what emerged from it as the regular and universally accepted order. So far I think it is true that we must judge of the earliest evidence in the light of its results, or in other words, that the authority of the church determines the form of the ministry.[5]

---

3. Lowrie, *The Church and Its Organization*, 339.
4. Gore, *Church and Ministry*, 9.
5. Gore, *Orders and Unity*, 83.

Gore's argument rests on these key points: (1) "the documents of the New Testament are only some of the documents which belong to a great historical movement," (2) "the earliest history must be interpreted in the light of what emerged from it as the regular and universally accepted order," and (3) "the authority of the church determines the form of the ministry."

First, Gore states that we do not rely solely on the New Testament for determining how the church is organized or for the definition of its officers. As we have seen in our survey, each congregation, from Pentecost to about 80 CE, determined its own structure; no uniform structure was imposed upon the various congregations until late in the first century. Gore admits as much when he states that, if we had no other record than the New Testament documents, we would be correct in assuming that "various tendencies" were at work in those centuries. No universal model of organization was imposed. Gore requires additional historic documents to establish the episcopacy. He admits he cannot do it with the New Testament alone.

For those opposed to the episcopacy, limiting the argument to the New Testament alone poses no problem. Documents like the *Didache* lift the veil slightly on how the ecclesiae organized themselves, how the prophetic ministry operated, and the reasons for its eclipse. But without them, the most we lose is that fuller detail. The essentials remain intact.

Next, Gore states that the proper ecclesiastical organization and authority in the church must be determined "by what emerged from it as the regular and universally accepted order." For Gore, the true form of ministry was determined by *universal* consensus and, because it emerged, it is valid. But emergence—even by consensus—does not prove validity in the theological realm. Mere emergence does not prove divine inspiration or providential safeguard. This is a problem that runs throughout the arguments by Gore, McLeod, Lightfoot, and others, who claim the episcopacy was a providential safeguard. One may not prove providential impetus or guidance by the mere fact that something emerged or survived. Furthermore, it is Gore's opinion that the episcopacy was universally accepted. Hatch disagrees, as we shall see.

But Gore's third statement is most significant of all. He claims that the authority of the church determines the true form of ministry—that what emerged was the "regular and universally accepted order" of the episcopacy. Since it was the authority of the church that caused it to emerge, it is the authority of the church that determines the proper form of ministry.

Gore will not allow that each congregation has the authority to self-organize, as it once did. He contends that the episcopacy—through apostolic succession—is the only proper ecclesiastical structure. Gore would have the church, through its only rightful authority—the successive and uninterrupted generations of ordained bishops—determine the acceptable form of ministry or ecclesiastical structure. Since only the bishops are successively ordained in the congregations, the bishops alone have the authority to determine ecclesiastical organization. Jesus commissioned the apostles who commissioned the bishops, and so on successively down the line. For a congregation today to have any other authority or organization, says Gore, is to oppose the divinely established ecclesiastical structure.

This is a variation of the argument from tradition, and it is essentially the same logic that permitted the development of the papacy. Traditional teaching determines truth—authority handed down by previous authority, which is determined to be truth by previous authority. Historic and successive tradition is equivalent to, if not supercedes, Scripture. It is strikingly similar to rabbinic arguments based on the "traditions of the elders."

Discussing the persistent demand by the Jews for the source of Jesus' teaching authority, Alfred Edersheim notes: "There [was] no principle more firmly established by universal consent than that *authoritative* teaching required previous authorization.... The ultimate appeal in cases of discussion was always to some great authority, whether individual Teacher or Decree by the Sanhedrin. And this was at least one aspect of the controversy between the chief authorities and Jesus."[6]

But the determination of truth can never be delegated to another person or group. The gift of discernment was one means in the ecclesia of testing for truth, but it was not limited to those with the gift. We are, as disciples, all *individually* responsible for *verifying* what we are taught. We are obligated to verify doctrine and question whether those "over us in the Lord" have a right to be in that position. No doctrine, no ecclesiastical authority is self-evident. We are obligated to test *everything* and discard what cannot be validated. This was a fundamental principle in the early ecclesiae. Ultimately, salvation is an individual and not a corporate responsibility.

6. Edersheim, 2:381.

Gore is familiar with this objection:

> Another idea has become characteristic of Protestantism, and especially of modern popular Protestantism . . . that "salvation" lies in a certain relation of the individual soul to God in Christ. It is obtained by faith in Christ. Faith is an act of the individual soul, and the believer receives the forgiveness of his sins and regeneration and the benefits of the new life simply because he individually believes in Christ. Those who thus believe and are saved find themselves bound in obedience to Christ to combine—for the ministry of the word and sacraments and for mutual assistance; but this combination into a visible fellowship in this world is a thing rather of secondary than of primary importance. The conditions under which believers in Christ combine among themselves can be arranged and re-arranged from time to time as they find most profitable to their spiritual life. There is no one obligatory organization or mode of combination. The one essential thing is the allegiance of the individual soul to Christ. By this fundamental faith the soul is already united to the only church which really matters—the invisible church of the elect—the blessed company of all faithful people. All else is a subsequent matter of voluntary organization. This is the doctrine of popular Protestantism. . . . This doctrine is, I venture to say, in glaring discrepancy with the New Testament as it stands.[7]

Gore believes that Scripture *and* tradition leave no room for self-organization by the congregation. He reverses the order and sees visible fellowship—the institution of the church—as primary and the individual as secondary. "The certain impression derived from the apostolic letters and the Acts is the impression that the salvation offered by Christ to man involves, and indeed consists in, membership in a society."[8] Gore sees uniformity as a necessary and essential part of unity and fellowship. He does not permit as valid models the independent, self-organized congregations that existed in the first century. Yet, Gore generously permits salvation to those opposed to this divine order.

> As God's love is not limited by His covenant, so He can work through ministrations which are not "valid"—that is, ministrations which have not the security of the covenant. But though God can do this, we have no right to claim it of Him. If He is not bound

---

7. Gore, *Orders and Unity*, 39–40.
8. Ibid., 47.

> to His sacraments, we men, up to the limits of our knowledge, certainly are. However excusable many may be in ignorance of divine institutions, we shall not be excusable if we are faithless to them for fear of hurting other men's feelings or disturbing existing arrangements.[9]

Wotherspoon concurs. He contends there are two conceptions of the church: (1) the church is antecedent to the individual—the Catholic view of the church, and (2) the individual is antecedent to the church—the individualistic or non-Catholic view of the church. Historically, those favoring the non-Catholic conception have had to argue from an a priori appeal for a distinction between the church as spiritual versus the church as institutional—a conception, he contends, that was not evident to all.[10]

> Its difficulties begin within sacred history—New Testament narrative and allusion seem to lend themselves more readily to the Catholic than to the individualistic reading. It can hardly be doubted that patristic evidence supports the Catholic theory, or that that has prevailed in the Church from a very early date. In order to hold any other theory it is necessary to suppose that the Church departed from its proper order within, if not before, the period known as sub-apostolic.[11]

But, as we have seen, that is precisely the verdict of history—the church departed from its proper order before the end of the first century.

For Gore, "the disentangling of tendencies and the emergence of dominant principles" provided the church with "regular and universally accepted order."[12] The church settled down "to run a longer course than it had at first expected."[13] The "the normal ministry or pastorate of souls as instituted by Christ in the church in the persons of the apostles and perpetuated by ordination out of the apostolic fount by succession" replaced the prophetic ministry.[14]

> There existed then, in the church from the first, by Christ's own disposition and appointment, in the persons of the apostles, officers

---

9. Gore, *Church and Ministry*, 92.
10. Wotherspoon, 3–7.
11. Ibid., 7.
12. Gore, *Orders and Unity*, 83.
13. Ibid., 109.
14. Ibid., 110–11.

> of government: commissioned stewards of the divine provisions made for men; pastors of the souls whom the Good Shepherd died to make His own. This appears both from S. Luke's writings and from the first and fourth Gospels. And when S. Paul, the apostle born out of due time, claims to be an apostle, commissioned by Christ Himself, equal to the original Twelve, he plainly claims, and is understood to claim, an office of pastoral authority, a "stewardship" for God, a "ministry of the new covenant", in the churches of his foundation and in the church at large.[15]

Gore emphasizes that, since the apostles were appointed by Christ himself, they were the stewards of divine provisions made for men. His unstated assumption is that those divine provisions included the sole legitimate authority to ordain their successors. His argument requires clear proof that (1) all congregations were organized under this principle and (2) all congregations acknowledged it. We will return to this momentarily.

Gore next considers *extra ecclesiam nulla salus* (outside the church there is no salvation).

> It is an unpalatable maxim and an untrue maxim if it is interpreted to mean that no one attains the end of man's being, or shares the ultimate or heavenly salvation—the membership in the kingdom of God which is to come—who is not a member of the church on earth. . . . None the less, Christ did come to establish a new covenant of salvation: a sphere of human life where God's salvation is known and accepted and realized here and now in the world: and this sphere of covenant is the visible society or church, into which men are admitted by the one baptism, and in which they profess in common the one name, and break the one bread, and submit to one rule of living, and know themselves to be members one of another.[16]

Reflecting on the first years after Jesus' death and resurrection, Gore argues that

> this picture of the beginning of the church in the Acts would make it necessary to assume that, before our Lord left the earth, He had given what we can only call official authority to the Twelve.[17]

---

15. Ibid., 93.
16. Ibid., 49–50.
17. Ibid., 88.

Gore maintains

> (1) that there was a ministry or stewardship instituted by our Lord in the church, and entrusted specially to the twelve apostles (and certainly also to S. Paul) who exercised it, under S. Peter's leadership at first, for the founding and maintenance of the church; (2) that this general ministry was shared by others beside the Twelve, whose authority we should gather was either given them by Christ on earth, like that of the Twelve, or was derived from the apostles by the laying on of hands, or was the authority of an acknowledged "prophet" probably certificated by miracles; (3) that the prophetic gift required recognition by the church and was to be exercised under the control necessary for the maintenance of the common order.[18]

Gore argues that the laying on of hands by the apostles, or those who received authority from them, was paramount in the transfer of authority.

> We may then take it as proved, by historical evidence of a cogent kind, that however the first ordinary local officers of the young Christian churches were designated for office, whether by prophecy pointing to them, or by the choice of the community—and we hear of both methods; their appointment was consummated from above, that is, from the superior authority of the apostles or apostolic men: that the method of appointment was by the laying on of hands with prayer; and that the idea attached to the laying on of hands, besides the idea of the commission of authority, was that also of the bestowal of the gift of the Spirit needed for the ministerial work.
>
> Moreover, when S. Paul was conscious that he was to leave the world by death, and that he had to make provision for a future which at first he had not anticipated, he shows himself, in his Pastoral epistles, very fully occupied with the task of giving permanence to the stewardship for God in the churches. Timothy and Titus are his appointed legates at Ephesus and in Crete: ordained by the laying on of hands: to fulfill the whole apostolic function of supervision, and specially the office of ordaining elders in the different churches entrusted to them. Thus, I do not see how it can be denied that the idea of an authoritative ministry instituted by Christ Himself in the persons of His apostles, and perpetuated out of the apostolic fount by delegation from above, through the laying on of hands, is confirmed in the New Testament; and that the

---

18. Ibid., 97–98.

rival idea of the churches appointing their own ministers by their own authority receives no confirmation at all.[19]

Gore finds proof of his argument in Acts 6:6, where the apostles lay hands on and commission the Seven—Philip being one of them. In Acts 8:17, Peter and John place their hands on the Samaritans and they received the Holy Spirit. In Acts 8:38, Philip baptizes the Ethiopian eunuch. In Acts 10:44–48, Cornelius and the others receive the Holy Spirit and are subsequently baptized. In Acts 11:22, when the church at Jerusalem hears of new believers in Antioch, it sends Barnabas down. Gore says:

> In Acts xiii.1–3 prophets (and teachers) appear as ministers of the Church's worship and they are represented as laying their hands after fasting and prayer upon Saul and Barnabas. On this occasion, however, the laying-on of hands recognized, rather than gave, apostolic commission, and a supernatural intimation led up to it; so that it was an exceptional event. But it is probable that those who could enact the rite on this occasion could have done so under more ordinary circumstances, for "ordination" or "confirmation."[20]

Gore argues that the element which connects all these events is the presence of someone in authority who is ordained—an authorized representative, commissioned either directly by Jesus or commissioned by those commissioned by Jesus. It is the presence of an authorized representative that validates and legitimizes the events. The apostles laid hands on the Seven; Peter and John laid hands on the Samaritans; Philip, who received authority by virtue of his membership in the Seven, baptized the eunuch. It must be assumed that Peter delegated authority to an unnamed person or persons to baptize Cornelius and the others, since it appears he did not perform the act himself. And, when news reaches Jerusalem about believers in Antioch, Barnabas is dispatched by those in authority. When Agabus the prophet comes down from Jerusalem to Antioch to warn of the impending famine, Gore requires that Agabus had been previously commissioned or ordained in the same way—either directly by Jesus or by those whom he appointed with the authority to commission. Gore permits the possibility that Agabus may have received direct ordina-

---

19. Ibid., 99–101.
20. Gore, *Church and Ministry*, 354.

tion by the Holy Spirit and, therefore, did not need apostolic commission or ordination. But Agabus has authoritative commission nonetheless.

In each case, Gore argues for ordination or commission only at the hands of those with the authority to commission or ordain. Although, in theory, he permits direct or supernatural ordination or commission, he clearly implies that it normally came through succession.

Since Gore permits at least the possibility that some individuals might receive commission directly from Jesus, no difference exists between what he permits and what the prophetic ministry claimed from the beginning. The prophets were commissioned either by a local, independent ecclesia or directly by the Holy Spirit, with some form of attestation—that is, either by the local congregation, through the gift of discernment, or else some other evidentiary sign. The record does not insist that *all* prophets were directly commissioned by the Holy Spirit, but that all were attested in some way. The fact that some members of the prophetic ministry may have received commission through the laying on of hands by their congregation does not force the conclusion that ordinary means replaced the special or miraculous.

The only way Gore can escape this problem is to assume that the special gifts have been withdrawn from the church. He *must* assume this for the sake of his argument on succession and ordination. If the special gifts have been withdrawn, direct ordination by the Holy Spirit is no longer possible, since supernatural attestation has ceased. This is why those who support the episcopacy must also deny the continuation of the miraculous or supernatural gifts. We will look at that argument in the next chapter.

Gore sees the fading of the prophetic ministry (he denies it was suppressed) as a natural attempt to bring predictable order to an organization under attack by false prophecy, heresy, and persecution. For him, the "ebbing away" of the prophetic ministry is providential. Gore sees potential danger if each congregation must continually test the prophetic utterance. For him, apostolic succession—ordination only by those previously ordained—is security and stability for the church.

Gore's final appeal is from the "father of the episcopacy" himself—Cyprian. Cyprian states that "there is a short way for religious and simple minds to lay aside error.... If the truth in any matter has been weakened or impaired, we may go back to the original of our Lord and His Gospel or to the apostolic tradition, and let the principles of our action take their rise there, where our order has its origin!"[21]

What is noteworthy about Cyprian's formula is that it also does not restrict this "fount" to the New Testament. Like Gore, Cyprian must include apostolic tradition. To do otherwise undermines his argument. By taking Cyprian at his word, and restricting our quest for the truth to the fount of "our Lord and His Gospel," apostolic succession collapses, leaving the prophetic ministry and the early organizational models standing.

Lowrie corrects Gore's idea of the church:

> But what stands first and foremost in Jesus' teaching about the conditions of membership in the Kingdom is the right attitude and behavior *towards God*; and the Church as a practical organization is made possible by no other bond than that of *brotherly love*, exhibiting itself in mutual comfort and edification. . . . [Jesus] never defined his Church, nor laid down rules for its organization; but left his followers to learn its true character from the development which was conditioned by the very fact of his Resurrection and Ascension, and from its subsequent progress under the guidance of the Spirit. . . . But that this power was bestowed upon [Peter] in his official capacity as apostle (or as chief of the apostles), there is no hint,—still less that it was an official prerogative which was meant to descend to an individual successor of Peter in the primacy of the Church (according to the Roman view), or to the bishops as representatives *in solidum* of the episcopate of Peter (according to the doctrine of Cyprian). On the contrary, we see from John 20:22, 23 and Matt. 18:17–20 that this power is given to the disciples as such and to the Church as a whole:—to every one that confesses a like faith with Peter, and, as a living stone, is built into the same edifice.[22]

Lindsay's contention is that, while there must be a valid ministry of some sort, this does not mean that authority must exist in a class or caste of superior office-bearers—nor can any such authority be delegated by the congregation. There is no succession of authority or office.[23]

Hatch concurs with both Lowrie and Lindsay in one respect. "The distinctions Paul makes between Christians are based not upon office, but upon varieties of spiritual power."[24] "The 'communion of saints' upon

---

21. Gore, *The Church and Ministry*, 57–58.
22. Lowrie, *The Church and Its Organization*, 112, 116, 123.
23. Lindsay, viii–x.
24. Hatch, 121.

which all Churches are built—is not the common performance of external acts, but a communion of soul with soul and of soul with Christ."[25]

Yet Hatch is inclined toward both the episcopacy and a separate, ordained class of officers, but he does not see events the same way Gore sees them. Hatch says that the theory that the confederation of churches were the visible and earthly form of the universal church is "attended with difficulties," to wit: (1) there is no proof the confederation was ever complete, (2) there is no proof the terms of the confederation were ever settled, and (3) there is no proof that the holy Scriptures—expressed or implied—refer to the unity of organization.[26] He notes the idea of unity underwent transformation: from (1) a changed life—common ideal, common hope, to (2) a belief as a basis of union—creeds, to (3) a unity of organization—dioceses.[27]

Many have argued that the episcopacy has value, even if it cannot be proved as Gore would have it. Hatch, for example, attempts to justify the rise of the institutional church based on its stabilizing effect in the midst of the collapsing Roman society surrounding it—as society deteriorated, the diocese kept it banded together.[28] The church became the only powerful organization in the civilized world after the disintegration of the Roman Empire. It became the visible realization of the kingdom of God, outside of which there was no salvation.[29]

Others have argued that the hierarchy of the church is a natural and practical process of adaptation. Hort, for example, sees the rise of the bishopric and the institutionalization of the church as a practical consequence of the experiences and circumstances that the church endured. But he emphatically denies "any ordinances on this subject were prescribed by the Lord, or that any such ordinances were set up as permanently binding by the Twelve or by St Paul or by the Ecclesia at large."[30] Hatch states that "the history of the organization of Christianity has been in reality the history of successive readjustments of form to altered circumstances."[31]

25. Ibid., 192.
26. Ibid., 184–87.
27. Ibid., 187–89.
28. Hatch, 164.
29. Ibid., 182.
30. Hort, 230.
31. Hatch, 218.

He adds: "In ecclesiastical—as in other human affairs—the ideal yields to the practicable."[32] Lightfoot takes a different approach: "Some representation is as necessary in the Church as it is in popular government."[33] Yet, he generously permits the possibility of circumstances demanding an alternative form: "An emergency may arise when the spirit and not the letter must decide."[34]

But these are all side issues. The real issue, as set out at the beginning of the chapter, is whether the evidence supports apostolic succession and the episcopacy as *ordained by God*—the only commissioned form of ecclesiastical government. Many are the champions of a special, ordained class within the congregations—a class commissioned as the sole, legitimate intermediaries between the common laity and Christ. But the conjecture of the episcopacy requires both tradition and extra-Biblical records to validate its legitimacy. The New Testament alone is not sufficient.

Hence, we may conclude with confidence that Jesus never specified how the congregations were to be organized, much less that there is proof of either apostolic succession or the episcopacy.

---

32. Ibid., 125.
33. Lightfoot, 134.
34. Ibid.

8

Excursus on the Supernatural Gifts

AUTHORITY WAS ONE OF the five characteristics, or marks, of the ecclesia, according to Lindsay. The presence and possession of the "gifts of the Spirit" was "the evidence of the presence of Jesus within the community, and gave the brotherhood divine authority to exercise rule and oversight in the absence of any authoritative formal prescriptions about a definite form of government."[1]

Paul lists some of these supernatural gifts or "gifts of the Spirit," emphasizing they are given to the ecclesia for the benefit of all.

> Now there are diversities of gifts, but the same Spirit. And there are diversities of ministrations, and the same Lord. And there are diversities of workings, but the same God, who worketh all things in all. But to each one is given the manifestation of the Spirit to profit withal. For to one is given through the Spirit the word of wisdom; and to another the word of knowledge, according to the same Spirit: to another faith, in the same Spirit; and to another gifts of healings, in the one Spirit; and to another workings of miracles; and to another prophecy; and to another discernment of spirits; to another kinds of tongues; and to another the interpretation of tongues: but all these works the one and the same Spirit, dividing to each one severally even as he will. (1 Cor 12:4–11 ASV)

For the early believers, the supernatural gifts were essential. Today, however, their absence—or presumed absence—is often said to be of no consequence. Those who vigorously defend the cessation of the supernatural gifts claim that they were merely a temporary expedient. Yet, given their importance and value to the early congregations, attempts to eliminate,

---

1. Lindsay, 113.

minimize, or otherwise invalidate those supernatural gifts undermine the very nature of the ecclesia.

It must be admitted that the book of Acts presents an obvious problem for Western Christians—especially new believers. Luke portrays events that create an uncomfortable contrast between the ecclesiae of the first century and the church today. What immediately strikes the modern reader is that the Spirit of Messiah was dramatically present and active amongst those early believers. Today, no one is bold enough today to claim that the miraculous *never* occurs, but it certainly seems less conspicuous than it appears to have been in those early years. Gore simply states the gifts "have not been usual in the church."[2]

Apologists have attempted to explain this disparity since the second century. Explanations would be totally unnecessary, if it were clearly stated anywhere in the New Testament that the miraculous would eventually cease. We naturally expect some indication by the authors of the New Testament that they knew those powers were transitory and would end at some point in the future. Because no explicit statement is made, many believers are compelled to believe that the miraculous must still be present in our time. But this is an argument from silence and is generally fallacious or weak.[3]

Briefly, those who support the cessation of the miraculous and the "special gifts" in the church generally contend that they were needed in the formative years of the church, but are no longer required. While they were present, miracles and the supernatural gifts served to confirm the authority of the apostles and establish the truth of the gospel. Others would add that the miraculous gifts were needed until the New Testament was complete.[4] But once confirmation was achieved or established, and the New Testament was complete, supernatural manifestation was no longer necessary and was withdrawn. God has done his part, so to speak. Anyone who claims that miraculous powers are still present is misled—or

---

2. Gore, *Orders and Unity*, 109.

3. However, under special circumstances—and in concert with other facts—silence can add weight to an argument.

4. There is a curious aspect to this line of argument. When *exactly* was the New Testament complete? Was it complete when it was finally delimited, or when its authors were finished writing? There are problems using either answer to support the cessation of the miraculous gifts. In a similar vein of specious reasoning, I have met individuals who will state emphatically that the final warnings in Revelation 22:18–19 apply to the entire Bible because Revelation is the last book in the Bible.

worse. Although no one is willing to deny that God *can* still intervene, no further evidence is necessary or should be sought. We walk by faith alone.

Gore deals with the cessation of the special gifts and their replacement by what he designates the "normal gifts" this way:

> There were specially inspired individuals in the earliest church called prophets: and in certain churches a somewhat general diffusion of special gifts of spiritual inspiration, whether prophecy or tongues or interpretation of tongues, which tended speedily to disappear; and as these special gifts of inspiration were withdrawn or suspended, the special teaching authority of the normal ministry of the church comes into greater prominence.[5]

Gore contrasts so-called special gifts with those administrative gifts used to organize the church:

> Doubtless, the brilliant display of personal, self-evidencing spiritual gifts threw into the shade the gifts which would naturally be associated with the words "helps" and "governments" in S. Paul's list of Corinthian endowments—the gifts of "deacon" and "presbyter", that is the ordinary gifts of administration.... But those special gifts did in fact prove transitory. They cannot be procured at will. They have not been usual in the church. You hear much of them at the beginning of the Acts and in the Epistle to the Corinthians. There is little of them in the Pastoral Epistles. Meanwhile the church was settling down to run a longer course than it had at first expected. It needed officers. It had officers from the first in the apostles, with others reckoned as prophets, or teachers, or evangelists.... What took place was that the exceptional or miraculous endowments of the earliest church passed into the background, and that the normal gifts of government and administration, which had always been existing and exercised by the apostles and their subordinates, came more and more into the foreground. The list in the Epistle to the Ephesians is more normal than that in the Corinthians.[6]

Gore has divided gifts a priori into two categories, special and ordinary, which is essential to his argument. He and others argue that the special gifts have been withdrawn, suspended, or passed away because we do not regularly see them now. But the weakness of such an argument is that it is

---

5. Gore, *Orders and Unity*, 2.
6. Ibid., 108–10.

completely empirical. A thing is not, or cannot be, because, so far as I am aware, it is not. This presumes, of course, that I have all the data to make such a declaration.[7]

Gore attempts to prove the miraculous endowments were temporary by their absence from most of Acts and the apostolic letters, or from what he has determined are later documents. He contends that, because a specific event or idea is not consistently or routinely mentioned or addressed, it is no longer relevant, significant, or present—which is, again, an argument from silence. But his argument is weak because it is not true to life. Paul's letters were written to those readers who received them, and address only those events or topics relevant to the needs of that hour.[8] This explains why letters are *never* universal in scope or detail, as Gore suggests they should be. Because something is not specified by Paul does not imply it does not exist. Some things may be assumed without being stated. Thus, silence can lend support both sides of an argument, as it does here. But Gore's argument hardly proves the supernatural powers were no longer significant, present, or were on their way out.

One attempted explanation by Wotherspoon deserves special notice. In contrast to Gore, he disagrees that the miraculous has been withdrawn. Instead, he posits a necessary evolution of God's supernatural expression. He begins his argument by employing an analogy of human muscles in training. When strengthened through physical exercise, muscles require less effort to accomplish the same task in the future. For Wotherspoon, the miraculous powers were that initial stage of training and were gradually replaced by a more mature, expanded capacity and energy. He concludes his argument by spiritualizing the issue.

> The later subsidence of "supernatural" demonstrations in the Church is due, not to the "passing away" of Spiritual power or to the withdrawal of any endowment, but on the contrary to the greater Spiritualisation of the Church and to its increasing capacity for correspondence with the Divine presence which is always seeking expression by its means. . . . The Divine Life appears less as a life operating independently within the Church, because it is now more thoroughly blent into the life of the Church itself; its force has passed into the ordinary channels of our activity and

---

[7]. Edersheim, 2:309.

[8]. Deissmann, 225. Deissmann addresses the pitfalls of forgetting the nature of letters.

> finds outlet through these.... As we watch subsidence of supranatural manifestation in the Christian Society we need not postulate change on the Divine side—the onrush of the Spirit continues as before ... an adaptation of the Body of Christ to that newly given Soul which is His Spirit, a gradual opening of its nerve paths to the stream of Christ's will, a gradual expansion of capacity in the organism to meet new demands; with a consequent direction of the new energy into its proper work of redeeming our humanity and of engaging it in the redemption of the world.... It may not as common incident sparkle in miracle or overwhelm startled souls to the point of ecstasy or trance. You must look now for its usual evidence in other forms ... in the work of faith and labour of love and patience of hope which appear in the lives of sinful men, or in the age-long vigilance and perennial vigour of the Church itself.[9]

Some may find his interpretation satisfactory; but it is a dubious attempt to circumvent a problem by spiritualizing it. His position is completely without scriptural support. Since he cannot find explicit scriptural support for the cessation of the gifts, he attempts to bring historic events in line with modern experience by spiritualizing the problem. But spiritualization is a dangerous methodology, even though it often allows the interpreter to stack the facts neatly. Because Scripture does not offer clear support does not license the interpreter to spiritualize the existing facts to achieve a conclusion he wants.

Generally, the argument that the special gifts passed away is built upon a presumption that those powers, at some time in the past, were usual, conspicuous, consistent, and predictable. Otherwise, how could we ever judge they had passed away? That presumption is both true and false, depending upon perspective. From our modern perspective and experience, those powers do seem to have been more usual, conspicuous, consistent, and predictable. In our time, the terminally ill are generally not healed, the dead are not raised, and demoniacs are either denied to exist or are treated with pharmaceuticals. Thus, because miracles are no longer evident to us, on our terms, or as we expect, we believe that the supernatural gifts have diminished or been withdrawn.

Certainly, during Jesus' earthly ministry, miracles were conspicuous, in that they were dramatic and performed before witnesses. A miracle is always conspicuous to those who witness it. His miracles also seem

---

9. Wotherspoon, 94–95.

to us consistent, until we remember that they were always tied to his reception and the faith of those who heard him (Matt 13:58). The New Testament documents do not support the notion that the miraculous was ever consistent or expected, by either those who witnessed it or by those at whose hands it took place. The disciples did not expect miracles in the company of Jesus—even when they had repeatedly seen them occur. They witnessed how Jesus fed thousands from meager provisions, yet did not presume he could or would do it again in similar circumstances shortly afterward. Those at Pentecost were not expecting to speak as they did. Peter did not expect to be released from prison through miraculous intervention. Neither did Paul and Silas. Even those instances where Luke writes of numerous miracles (Acts 2:43; 5:12; 6:8; 14:3; 15:12; 19:11) do not prove they were consistent or predictable. He simply chooses not to catalogue them individually. The only thing that seems consistent in the New Testament is the amazement of the witnesses to those miracles.

There were also occasions when the miraculous was apparently withheld. Stephen (Acts 7:58–60) and James (Acts 12:2) were not saved through supernatural interposition from violence and death. Paul's "thorn" was not removed. Furthermore, we find other occasions when we would have expected supernatural powers to have been deliberately exercised, if they were indeed procured by the disciples at will. In the cases of Epaphroditus (Phil 2:26–27), Timothy (1 Tim 5:23), and Trophimus (2 Tim 4:20), the record implies that time and natural means restored these individuals to health.[10]

In addition to our confused understanding and expectations of the supernatural gifts, we must admit that we are also in the habit of minimizing or redefining the miraculous. The simple answer to prayer for needed funds to pay bills, when we have no other means, or the salvation of someone after years of consistent and careful prayer do not seem very miraculous when compared to healing the terminally ill or raising the dead. So we define and rank for ourselves what is miraculous or supernatural intervention and what is not.

When we assume that miracles were usual, consistent, expected, or procured on demand, we are reading that into the New Testament, because those events appear more conspicuous than our experience. Yet, there was no predictability in those times, just as there is no predictability

---

10. Yet, we must tread with caution here—that implication may be incorrect.

now. And it is foolish to certainly conclude that they have passed away on that basis alone. It is a misrepresentation of the historic record.

Irenaeus, who died about 202 CE, did not believe the gifts were transitory, although he clearly indicates they were never usual.

> It is not by invocation of angels, nor by incantations, nor by any other presumptuous act that [the church] performs these works, but by having a pure mind and clean hands, and by honestly directing her prayers to the Lord Who made all things, and by invoking the name of our Lord Jesus Christ she wrought miracles for the weal of men and not for the making of proselytes.[11]

His comment brings up an interesting point—which, as it turns out, is the lesson of the entire New Testament. Irenaeus insists that the miraculous gifts in the ecclesia were bestowed for the benefit of the congregation and its members, and occurred according to the circumstance and the needs of the body—in its activity for the kingdom of God. It is that lesson which is the fundamental issue.

Brother Andrew was trained to expect God's provision when in God's service. He relates in *God's Smuggler* more than a dozen episodes of miraculous intervention, provision, protection, rescue, and healing while preparing for and transporting Christian literature into communist countries—each one just as extraordinary as those mentioned in the New Testament. The organization, Gospel for Asia, regularly cites testimony of supernatural interposition from its missionaries. As the gospel spreads over India and China today, new believers in those countries would certainly disagree that the miraculous gifts have been withdrawn. Lindsay noted a century ago that the most illustrative examples of the early church are to be found in the mission field.[12] Are these believers in India and China, or others engaged in kingdom work, deluded by their own exuberance and enthusiasm?

Jesus linked the miraculous endowments to faith (trust), prayer, and *kingdom service*. The promise Jesus makes to his disciples (John 14:12–14) is tied to work for the gospel and kingdom. Those who performed healings and exorcisms, or were miraculously protected or provided for, were dedicated, one and all, to service for the kingdom. The kingdom was their life.

11. Hitchcock, 260.
12. Lindsay, xi.

If the miraculous is not conspicuous today, it is because our focus is wrong. Jesus taught that we must put the kingdom *first* and make it our life. *Only then* we could expect God's provision and miraculous intervention. But first means exactly that. Instead, we rush around, accumulating possessions and money, storing up for ourselves, making plans to do this or that—oh yes, and attending church—and then wonder why the miraculous does not seem to occur as it did in the first century. In fact, we have come to not expect the miraculous—nor should we. Messiah is not our first source of help. Instead, we seek His intervention only when all other means have failed. Why should we expect anything from someone we do not trust, who is not the central focus of our lives, and whom we do not truly work for?

Hollow disciples claim to follow Messiah, call him Lord, but do not do what he says. Hollow disciples expect what Jesus only promised to those who deny themselves and devote their lives wholeheartedly to the mission of the gospel and the kingdom.

Perhaps the miraculous has not been withdrawn at all. Rather, like the prophetic ministry, it has been *eclipsed*—still available, but inaccessible because our direction, dedication, and focus is wrong. Miracles were an evidence of apostleship (2 Cor 12:12), but were also given to the ecclesiae as a whole, to bestow authority and to show that Jesus was present with them.

Apostles were not the sole possessors of the supernatural gifts. To limit the supernatural gifts to the apostolic age—to the Twelve or Paul or any of the other apostles of that generation—is untenable. In Paul's mind, apostles were apostles—he rejects rank in apostleship (2 Cor 12:11). An apostle was proved to be so by attestation.

When the prophetic ministry—the apostles and prophets—receded by determination of the local ministry, the supernatural gifts and spiritual power of the ecclesiae also receded, until eventually Chrysostom (c. 347–407 CE) could deny that the miraculous gifts still existed in the church.[13]

---

13. In his Twenty-Ninth Homily on First Corinthians, Chrysostom states: "the miraculous gifts are no more." James Hoppin notes: "The simple reason he gives for this is, that the circumstances of the times were changed. When men were converted out of rank heathenism, in order that they might know the truth, and teach it to others, and confirm it by their works, they were straightway endowed with supernatural powers; and they had to be possessed of these powers to contend with the pretended miraculous powers of the heathen soothsayers. So long as Christianity had to encounter the reign of devils on earth, Chrysostom says, its miraculous gifts were continued" (Hoppin, 42–43). In a

If the church—like Israel—rejected God's provision for the congregations through the prophets, and chose instead what it thought a wiser course, it is reasonable and scripturally sound to expect that it deliberately cut off that power and blessing—just as Israel did.

But to claim that the supernatural gifts were a temporary expedient, and were never meant to be permanent, is to deny a fundamental tenet of the early ecclesia: the gifts were testimony of the presence and authority of Messiah in the ecclesia.

---

word, Chrysostom's argument has teeth only if the reign of devils on earth has ceased.

9

Recapitulation

Until the last decade of the first century, the Christian congregations were loosely organized with a twofold ministry: the prophetic ministry, consisting of apostles and prophets, and the local ministry, consisting of a collegiate body of elders and deacons. These two groups were not mutually exclusive. The prophetic ministry, when present in the congregation, was received as a higher authority only after it had passed discernment by the congregation. The prophetic ministry bound the ecclesiae together and edified the congregations through apocalypses and insight into the Scriptures. The local ministry cared for the practical needs of the community.

Each ecclesia was an independent "tiny island in a sea of surrounding paganism"[1] and was free to organize itself as it chose. The congregations held three distinct meetings for edification and worship, thanksgiving with a communal meal, and its business affairs. The apex of worship was the communal meal, or Agape, that concluded with the Lord's Supper.

The early Christians were circumspect about their lives amidst the surrounding pagan society. They focused on caring for each other and putting their profession of faith into practice through the sharing of their worldly wealth with brethren in need. The wealthier members viewed their wealth as a gift from God for the provision of the congregation, and not for selfish purposes. The Two Ways was an attempt to clarify proper from improper conduct. Early believers were careful to give no offense to the gospel, to refuse participation in any form of wrath or judgment, or indecent amusements or speech. Believers examined how they earned their living, whether it was in keeping with what they professed, and aban-

1. Lindsay, 57.

doned it, if it was in conflict. They removed the slightest hint of paganism from their daily lives, at the cost of derision, poverty, or even death. They considered themselves sojourners—alien residents. The congregation provided encouragement and support in this struggle, as they awaited the return of their Savior.

Before the end of the first century, and shortly after the deaths of the original shepherds of that generation, a silent and virtually uncontested revolution altered the structure and leadership of the ecclesiae. Faced with the dual attacks of heresy and persecution—and the perceived dangers they imposed—the local ministry of bishops, elders, and deacons displaced the authority of the prophets and apostles. The prophetic ministry was eclipsed by and made subservient to the local ministry. From that point on, the prophetic ministry was judged not on its message, as it had been, but on its total obedience to the authority and doctrine of local ministry.

In the short span of fifty years, the prophetic ministry, though acknowledged in theory, faded in practice. The local ministry (the collegiate session of elders and deacons) elevated a single man (the bishop) to rule over them. The contrivance of apostolic succession implied that the bishop had received the laying on of hands from those who had received it from the original apostles. The acceptance of this fiction permitted the bishop to become the sole repository of both doctrine and discipline. Only through the laying on of his hands were the gifts of the Holy Spirit dispensed. The Agape was eliminated and replaced by the Eucharist, which was transmuted into a sacrifice. Only in the bishop's presence and by his authority was the Eucharist legitimately celebrated. The bishops successfully defended themselves against the attempt to revive the prophetic ministry and the attempt by the martyrs to overrule their authority. Eventually, only the bishop could pronounce pardon. Where the bishop was, there was the church.

Even before persecution by the state ended, the bishops sought to unify all congregations in both doctrine and organization. The congregation was divided into two distinct castes—the clergy and the laity. Doctrine changed as well. As masses of former pagans flooded the churches, doctrine was relaxed. Christianity absorbed many of the elements of paganism and the imperial cult. After Christianity was legalized, those isolated congregations that had managed to retain the old structure or held alternative doctrine were forced to conform to established orthodoxy and practice by imperial fiat. When Christianity became the religion of the Roman state, and the revenues of the pagan temples were surrendered to the bishops, the clergy received annual salaries, and the church became the dominant force of Roman society. The bishops shared power with the state and declared that no means of salvation existed outside the established, catholic, institutional church.

Once grasped, power and authority is seldom surrendered voluntarily.

We now have ample facts to answer the question posed obliquely in the introduction to this survey: Is the institutional church the same church that Jesus established? I contend it is not. The contrast in organization and doctrine is far too disparate and significant to claim otherwise. And there is little, if any, similarity between the daily walk of the early Christians—their conduct amidst a pagan culture—and what is called Christian life today.

The historical evidence, therefore, permits the following four conclusions:

1. The eclipse of the prophetic ministry by the local ministry, and the subsequent transformation of the ecclesia into the institutional church, was an attempt to build and protect from harm that which was always in the Lord's care. It was humans' attempt to be wiser than God.

2. Those with ecclesiastical oversight taught that Christians could comingle with the surrounding society without jeopardizing their faith. They permitted syncretism in the belief that whatever the church blesses may be used in service to Christ.

3. Apostolic succession, the episcopacy, and the clergy-laity distinction are all legal fictions. No spiritual rank or status was ever intended to exist in the church. The non-ordained believer is not suspect.

4. No single individual was ever intended to be responsible for instruction or edification in the ecclesia. The congregation was never expected to support its local ministry. A salaried pastorate is unscriptural and the product of later embellishments.[2]

---

2. I recommend an obscure work by James Beaty, *Paying the Pastor Unscriptural and Traditional*. He tackles the subject completely and with clarity. One point is worthy of reproduction here. Commenting on the "man of lawlessness" in 2 Thess 2:7, he writes: "It is remarkable not only from the peculiar and extraordinary characteristics indicated

For reasons that should now be clear, we have the right to assert that the word *church*, as it is used today, means an entity that possesses *at least one* of the following defining qualities:

1. It supports at least one authoritative member by a regular stipend or salary.
2. It owns property as an entity.
3. It segregates members into two groups of ordained and non-ordained, each of which has specified or implied rank or function.
4. It has no prophetic ministry.

In most cases today, all four defining qualities apply. In the first century, none applied—until after the prophetic ministry was eclipsed.

These are disturbing facts, and it is natural to deny their validity or significance. "We take that to be true which we should like to have so, and ideas that go contrary to our hopes and wishes have difficulty in getting lodgment."[3] Still we might be able to find refuge in a couple of excuses. If being a Christian means simply acknowledging the atonement of the cross, being baptized, and then attempting to do the best we can in our current circumstances, we are excused. Or, if the daily conflicts of those early believers were nothing but the result of the initial confrontation between paganism and Christianity—as many believe—and Christian life and doctrine were intended to evolve with and adapt to the surrounding culture, we are also excused. If either is the case, we may admire the conduct and resolve of those early believers without feeling any shame or inadequacy.

But it seems that we are permitted neither. The New Testament does not teach that we are to do the best we can, or that we may accommodate the demands made by the culture that surrounds us. We are cautioned against conforming to the world (Rom 12:2 is but one example). We are exhorted to be on guard against all forms of syncretism and carefully examine our lives. The Two Ways, a doctrinal foundation of the early eccle-

---

to be subsequently manifested in opposition to the religion of Christ, but more particularly from the fact that it would actually manifest itself or be revealed in the body of Christ—the temple of God. . . . That was a "mystery" in his time, a stealthy, mysterious violation of positive law, that would develop the most stupendous organizations of lawlessness, disobedience, and iniquity that the world ever trembled under" (Beaty, 12–13). In short, "the man of lawlessness" will arise from within the believing community. He will be an apostate believer.

3. Dewey, 28.

siae, is evident throughout Scripture and remains as relevant for us today as for the early congregations. To acknowledge that the early structures and doctrine were intended to be normal and perpetual means that we have fallen far short of the mark, to put it mildly. Yet, this failure and play-acting is hardly a recent development. It was evident seventeen centuries ago, as one event from Roman history will illustrate.

Julian "the Apostate"—an epithet that retains the odium of ecclesiastical historians[4]—was Constantine's nephew. From his youth, Julian studied Christian doctrine at the feet of royal theologians and worshipped at the altar of Christ. But, at the age of twenty, he rejected Christianity. When he became emperor of the Roman Empire in 360 CE, Julian removed Christians from the military and all judicial and public offices, to which they had grown accustomed, reminding them "that it was unlawful for a Christian to use the sword either of justice or of war." And, to ensure their compliance, he "studiously guarded the camp and the tribunals with the ensigns of idolatry."[5] He directed the bishops to restore to their former owners all the lands, property, and revenue of those pagan temples that Constantine had ceded to the church. With a smile, he reminded the unhappy clergy that they were not supposed to be rich in the world's goods—like their Savior, they were to remain poor.[6] Even the pagan Julian understood the demands of the gospel long after the bishops and clergy had conveniently forgotten them.

It seems the curse of humanity is to repeat sin as well as history. When Israel entered the land, it did not drive out the inhabitants, as Jehovah had commanded (Exod 23:33; Judg 2:1–2). Israel intermarried with the encompassing nations and lusted after their Ashtars and Baals (Judg 2:11; 3:6). Later still, Israel coveted an earthly king, like the nations around them (1 Sam 8:5). In spite of Samuel's warning of what a king would demand, Israel insisted (1 Sam 8:19). Jehovah acquiesced in anger (Hos 13:10–11). Israel did not want Jehovah to dwell amongst them in a portable tabernacle, as he had intended. They wanted to assign Jehovah

---

4. Historians often ignore that Julian reinstated religious toleration throughout the Roman Empire and recalled the bishops and clergy of those heretical sects banished by his uncle. He frequently invited Christian theologians to his palace and encouraged their angry disputations—believing that Christianity posed no threat so long as its votaries were content to devour each other.

5. Gibbon, 1:355–56.

6. Ibid., 1:359.

to a temple—a stationary edifice. Jehovah did not want an edifice (2 Sam 7:7), for Messiah would build the true temple (2 Sam 7:13). But, again, Jehovah acquiesced. Yet, even then Israel's sin was not complete. It continued its blatant idolatry and syncretism and, after repeated pleadings and warnings through the prophets, Jehovah removed them from the land and sent them into captivity.

Israel's profligacy is the sin of the church. Julian's condemnation remains valid today. Like Israel, the church has not driven away foreigners or paganism from its congregations. It has lusted after the Baals and Ashtars of worldly mammon, has desired earthly kings in the form of a separate and ordained class, or else has genuflected to worldly, political power. It does not want to be led by the prophetic ministry. It does not want Messiah or the kingdom—except on its own terms. And it crafts carefully reasoned arguments to justify those terms.

The original ecclesia was not a blueprint that was intended to be altered at the discretion of its leaders, just as the tabernacle was not a temporary expedient. As Howard Snyder points out, the tabernacle was Jehovah's design and symbol of what the ecclesia was to be. "The tabernacle is the symbol of God's presence with his people, and as such it is, supremely, a mobile symbol. Everything is made to be extremely easy to be dismounted and carried.[7] The three central elements in the Mosaic covenant were sacrifice, priesthood, and tabernacle.... The great temptation of the organized church has been to reinstate these three elements among God's people: to turn the community into an institution."[8] Neither the tabernacle nor the ecclesia were ever intended to be converted into an edifice.

The inescapable conclusion of this survey is that the prophetic ministry demanded too much effort and undermined the authority of the local ministry. But the attempt to order all things was achieved at a great price. In that sense, Israel's sin was prophetic for the church, and the church is in captivity today for the same reasons Israel was sent into captivity and exile.

---

7. Snyder, 61.
8. Ibid., 57–58.

10

Conclusion

Jeremiah declared that Jehovah brought Israel out of Egypt with signs and with wonders, with a strong hand, with an outstretched arm and with great terror, and gave them the land that he had sworn to their fathers. It was a land flowing with milk and honey. He reminds Israel that they came in and possessed it, but they did not obey Jehovah. As a result, Jeremiah says, Jehovah caused the invading evil to come upon them—he ordered them to be carried into captivity (Jer 32:21-23). Ezekiel too declares Israel's apostasy and the sin of its shepherds (Ezek 22:3-16; 34:2-10). Daniel rehearses Israel's deliberate disobedience (Dan 9:6, 10-13). Hosea notes Israel's rejection of truth (Hos 8:3-4, 7-8, 14; 10:1-4, 13). These are but a few oracles in the Old Testament that apply easily to the apostasy of the institutional church since the eclipse of the prophetic ministry in the first century.

The church has been in captivity since the end of the first century because its leaders rejected oversight by the prophetic ministry and trusted instead in the presumed wisdom of the local ministry. Spiritual deterioration and apostasy accelerated when those in authority accommodated the surrounding culture and united with the Roman state. They attempted to mix the unmixable. Institutional Christianity is the fruit of the human attempt to remedy what is considered imperfect or vulnerable. In that effort, Christians chose predictable order, rule, and authority instead of the spontaneous, convivial, and organic.

"At first," Moxom says, "Christianity existed without organization. The early Church was a plastic mass, without officers and without specific functions. . . . This mass of religious protoplasm, or life-stuff, with strong powers of assimilation, quickly became organic. The organization was at first extremely simple, elastic, and free. The exigencies of the situation, however, combined with the inevitable tendency of human nature, soon produced a marked change."[1]

The inevitable tendency of human nature is in conflict with the Holy Spirit. Indeed, direction by the Holy Spirit through the prophetic ministry is unsettling—it is unpredictable and requires that the ecclesia and believer, one and all, know Messiah well enough to discern false doctrine. When the ecclesiae encountered heresy, the simplest solution was to restrict, and then prohibit, the prophets and apostles, replacing them with ordained men who would teach consistent doctrine. When the church was finally secure in the bosom of the state, these same men were able to establish a united front against anything that deviated from the "truth handed down." We are the inheritors of their misguided efforts.

Edersheim remarks that "ceremonialism rapidly develops too often in proportion to the absence of spiritual life."[2] Institutionalism arises from similar causes. In *Deschooling Society*, Ivan Illich describes two characteristics of institutions, which are easily applied to the institutional church. Institutional Christianity operates on two basic illusions: (1) freedom and equality are found within its walls and (2) hierarchical organization is essential to the Christian life. But the institutional church has confused process with substance. The institutional church believes that escalation leads to success—the more structure that exists, the more efficiency.[3] Illich notes that institutionalization of values inevitably leads to "physical pollution, social polarization, and psychological impotence . . . modernized misery."[4]

The New Testament teaches that Christians have a right to a non-intermediary relationship with Messiah, yet the institutional church is destructive to that end through its use of ordination. Ordination is institutional segregation. Freedom in Messiah is thus redefined—through a legal fiction—to mean recognizing and being under the authority of its ordained officers. The ordained know what is best because they are ordained—hands have been placed upon them, as they have been successively placed upon those before them, back to the earliest times. Whether stated this way or not, this conception applies to any ecclesiastical gov-

1. Moxom, 52-53.
2. Edersheim, 2:492.
3. Illich, 1.
4. Ibid., 1-2. While Illich's paradigm is not entirely transferable to institutional Christianity, it is amazing how much actually is.

ernment that obtains its leaders through institutional ordination. But this notion is specious because all doctrinal persuasions cannot possess the unbroken line of truth—and each declares the others heterodox.

Instead of the loosely organized, independent congregations of the early years, a separate, ordained leadership caste dispenses homogeneous doctrine and all necessary discipline to ensure it. Those outside this caste are the uninformed and subservient. Remarkably, this was the state of Judaism in the first century, when the Jews were either members of the established order or else what the Pharisees and Sadducees designated the *'am ha-arets*—the ignorant country people.

The ordained hierarchy of Judaism repeatedly demanded to know from Jesus the source of his authority (Luke 20:2). "Who ordained you? Where is your 'succession'? Where are your credentials?" Their question was legitimate—it was *the most important question*, because, without proof of succession and ordination, there was no right to teach authoritatively. Credentials elevated a distinct class that was spiritually and intellectually superior to other men.

But Jesus ignored their demand. Instead, he claimed his words and deeds alone were evidence of his right to teach authoritatively and proved that he was who he claimed to be (Luke 7:22). Those who recognized his words and deeds as truth also recognized the origin of his authority—for fruit always shows the nature of the tree.

Thus, we may legitimately ask: What is the fruit of the institutional church and its ordained caste?

The church is supposed to liberate and mature its members for service. Instead, it perpetuates a need for itself by keeping its members in a perpetual state of immaturity, which is the goal of any institution.[5] The church creates consumer-Christians, whose only function is to absorb what its ordained leaders determine is legitimate. With few exceptions, it fosters believers who continually crave milk, or it coddles them and encourages them to lead lives of syncretism, instead of encouraging spiritual growth and independence that leads to separation from the world.

The ordained or clergy class has monopolized and expropriated discernment with the full—if not enthusiastic—approval of the non-ordained. The clergy has the sole power to determine legitimate from illegitimate, and anything that is deemed illegitimate or suspect is prohib-

---

5. See Illich, "Why We Must Disestablish Schools," in *Deschooling Society*, 1–24.

ited. Once members accept the logic that the ordained have the sole right to determine legitimate from illegitimate, they gladly accept the very idea of the laity class and are forced to conform to established structure and values. Anything contrary to established structure and values is deemed illegitimate and may even be cause for discipline.

The church prepackages the service and function of its members and clearly communicates the boundaries that members may not cross. The ordained hierarchy establishes rank and function to all its members—clergy or laity. Each has function and rank.[6] Believers surrender their independent relationship to Messiah and accept oversight by the ordained.

For their part, people have historically preferred intermediaries, because intermediaries alleviate the need for individual responsibility. Intermediaries remove the fearful responsibility of an individual relationship with Messiah—in the same way Israel cried out to Moses, "Speak to Jehovah for us! For, if we see Him, we will die!" (Exod 20:19). In place of individual accountability, church members are encouraged to demand ceremony, ritual, and tradition—elements that leave members feeling comfortable and secure, but which produce "cheesecake Christians"[7]—soft and sweet, but lacking substance.

The institutional church has relegated the work of the Holy Spirit to a quaint notion. It readily accepts the *theory* of the presence of the Holy Spirit, but it no longer believes the Holy Spirit has any practical, immediate power to direct, protect, or correct the assembly—unless it passes through the hands of the ordained. The Holy Spirit no longer abides in the center of the congregation. Instead, it directs by proxy. The salaried[8] and ordained pastor, the church board, the presbytery, or the consistory direct congregational life and perpetuate the fantasy that *it is the Holy Spirit who is directing the congregation through them*. The non-ordained members are continually reassured they are receiving correct doctrine, and are thus tranquilized.

6. Directly applied from Illich's paradigm of the institution of schools.

7. I thank my daughter, Sam, for introducing me to this expression.

8. "There is not an instance in the New Testament of any service in the congregation of Christ, of any kind, ever having been paid for with the approval of the Holy Spirit speaking through the Apostles. This will appear strange in an age in which the 'door will not be shut for nought;' and when it can be said, as was said of Zion of old, 'The heads thereof judge for reward, and the priests thereof teach for hire, and the prophets thereof divine for money: yet will they lean upon the Lord, and say, 'Is not the Lord among us? none evil can come upon us' (Mic 3:11)" Beaty, 83.

Spiritual gifts must also pass through the hands of the ordained. The ordained dispense those gifts they deem appropriate, or else label them nonexistent, unnecessary, or suspect. The prophetic ministry is labeled illegitimate because it is spontaneous and unpredictable—and what is unpredictable is suspect or dangerous.

Ostracizing any member of the ecclesia who deliberately refuses to repent is a legitimate use of the keys that Jesus transferred from the rabbis to the congregation. Although the early ecclesiae ostracized members for repeated and unrepentant sin, the institutional church excommunicates for questioning authority or doctrine. At the hands of Roman troops, the church has systematically hunted down and surrendered to the sword or flames all those who would oppose its doctrine or authority—all in the cause of a warrior Messiah, an avenger of those who would oppose the church. Believers today continue to be warned not to speak against the Lord's prophet—conveniently and ironically redefined to mean the pastor, the ordained, or the clergy.

During the Protestant Reformation, while Calvinists and Lutherans were busy hammering out the subtle intricacies of their doctrines, the Radical Reformers attempted to call the church back to its earliest form and life. Catholics and Protestants designated them *Anabaptists* (rebaptizers), because of their opposition to infant baptism. For them, salvation was purity of life, not whether one's creed or understanding of the finer points of theology were correct. The Radical Reformers believed the church had fallen into apostasy and wanted to return to the Christianity of the first century. They insisted that a believer's daily life must align with the gospel.

Menno Simons (1496–1561), Peter Riedemann (1506–1556), and other Radical Reformers recalled the early doctrines of the ecclesia— especially the Two Ways. They preached that believers have their citizenship in heaven; Christians are sojourners; like the Levites, they have no inheritance; they are resident aliens, migrants, temporary inhabitants in a foreign land, awaiting restoration. As such, they have no vested interest or part to play in any government, except to obey its laws, where those laws do not conflict with Scripture. They cannot vote, since they are not citizens and since it would be participatory nationalism. A Christian may not resist evil or be an instrument of wrath. Like the Levites, a Christian cannot serve in the military (Num 1:44l–47), for that would place a sword in his hand—hence, there can be no just war for true followers of Messiah.

Believers cannot serve on a jury, since that is participating in wrath and judgment. Neither may they bring a lawsuit, but instead, trust in the Lord's recompense. Believers have neither the authority nor an obligation to make any country a Christian nation or society. Instead, their lives are to be a living testimony—a message of salvation, mercy, pardon, and impending judgment.

The Radical Reformers expected that the Holy Spirit's work in their lives would ultimately result in communal living, as in the early days of the Jerusalem church. When this proved to be impractical or was made illegal, to foil their attempt, the Radical Reformers formed small groups of families living in close proximity, sharing their material resources. It was their fundamental belief that new life in Messiah was selfless.

The Radical Reformers recalled that a believer must carefully examine the way he earns his living, which must always be in keeping with the Spirit of Messiah. A believer must be completely honest and must never take advantage of another's misfortune. He may make a profit for real work only—a middleman's occupation is prohibited. Since governments are instruments of wrath and appointed by God for that purpose, believers cannot hold positions in them. A believer may not make his living in any way that might force him to judge, participate in enforcement of laws, participate in nationalism, or serve as a proxy of Caesar, since one cannot serve Jehovah and Caesar simultaneously. One cannot be of law and grace at the same time.

The Radical Reformers were determined to live as aliens in a foreign land and, at the same time, to be untainted by the surrounding culture. Both Protestants and Catholics despised them and attempted to expunge their radical notion that the church and the surrounding societies were separate.

It is noteworthy that the Radical Reformers taught that nothing indicated a believer's spiritual state more clearly than his relationship to money. Jesus had warned his followers of the inherent dangers of mammon—money and possessions—and how it choked the good seed. Mammon is to be used for righteous and not selfish purposes (Luke 16:9–13). A consistent theme throughout Scripture is that wealth brings arrogance, pride, apathy, and the eventual forgetting of Jehovah—certainly less dependence on him. Striving for financial and material success and accumulating money and possessions is not a kingdom principle. Contrary to

Western notions, wealth is no indication of Jehovah's blessing.[9] Instead, as we observed, the early principle was that wealthy members were given their wealth to share with those who were in need. Only in that way could wealth be a blessing. When Zaccheus parts with half his wealth and restores fourfold what he had obtained wrongfully, Jesus cites his actions as evidence of his salvation (Luke 19:8–9). The early believers applied this principle assiduously and opened their homes and sold their property so others might have what they needed.

It is false prophecy and an abomination to teach that "God helps those who help themselves"—to give license to those with money and possessions, as if their wealth is the result of their own toil (Deut 8:11–18). This is a hard teaching for Western Christians, who believe in error that Jesus died so that capitalism and individual opportunity to create wealth might flourish.

Real faith in Messiah demands that we submit to a new social arrangement. Devotion to Messiah demands practical devotion to the brethren. Those material comforts and necessities that we want and claim for ourselves, we must strive to provide for others.[10] Those rich in the world's goods are expected to provide for those in the community who lack them.[11] To deliberately turn away from or to concoct some nice argument that permits us to ignore someone in need is to disregard a fundamental teaching of the gospel (Jas 2:16–17).[12]

Eberhard Arnold writes in *Innerland*, "The prophetic spirit calls to account all who helped trample the poor, who sided with the rich against those with nothing. The prophet Amos says every luxury is won at the expense of the poor and needy. The wealthy enjoy expensive furnishings, rich food and drink, and spacious rooms only through tyrannizing and

---

9. When Jesus discusses wealth and its relation to salvation (Matt 19:23–25, Mark 10:17–31, Luke 18:24–26), the disciples' astonishment arises from the common Jewish misconception that wealth was indicative of Jehovah's favor.

10. Arnold, *Innerland*, 159.

11. Lindsay, 115.

12. Many who claim to follow Jesus have simply "come to Jesus" so that they might enjoy the promises of the restoration—or in the common parlance, "go to heaven." No change occurs in their behavior or attitudes. They continue on as they always have. They are believers in name only, as if they had purchased an eternal life-insurance policy. They have taken care of what happens after death, so to speak, and that is the sum of their salvation. Jesus repeatedly warned against this and stated frankly that such individuals are living an illusion. True salvation manifests real change in behavior and attitudes.

crushing the poor and needy. Other prophets too hurl their 'Woe betide thee!' at those who, by amassing clothing and furniture from the poor through seizure, become enemies of their own people: 'You tear the skin from the body and the flesh from the people's bones.' 'You feed upon the flesh of my people.' "[13]

As Edersheim notes, the parable of the foolish rich man indicates there is real danger in accumulating wealth.

> That part of the things which a man possesseth by which his life is sustained, consists not in what is superabundant; his life is sustained by that which he needs and uses; the rest, the superabundance, forms no part of his life, and may, perhaps, never be of use to him. Why, then, be covetous, or long for more than we need? And this folly also involves danger. For, the love of these things will engross mind and heart, and care about them will drive out higher thoughts and aims.[14]

The fundamental issue is greed—what Milton Friedman blithely redefined as self-interest. Greed is born of the spirit of mammon. But, mammon is far more than an abundance of possessions and money, as Arnold notes.[15] Mammon is the reduction of life to the material—it places a value on human life and separates one person from another. Property, wealth, and material possessions all belong to someone. What I have is mine and what you have is yours. What I have places a value on me, just as what you have places a value on you. The spirit of mammon teaches that we are what we possess—the more we own, the greater our worth. Those who have less are worth less, or may even be expendable.

Hence, mammon must be protected. It was the spirit of mammon that created laws ensuring the right of the individual to protect wealth and property, the right to take up the sword—physically or legally—to make certain no one takes from us what is ours. This is exactly how a just war is conceived. It begins with the principle that I have rights to my wealth and my land, and I may defend it by the sword, if necessary. This is serving mammon, and this, too, is a hard teaching.

Another principle born of the spirit of mammon is the belief that one must set aside money against some unseen calamity. Western Christians

---

13. Arnold, *Innerland*, 260.
14. Edersheim, 2:243.
15. Arnold, *Salt and Light*, 146.

especially see the "safety net" principle as sound and responsible. Yet, this principle is erected on the mistaken idea that we need to concern ourselves with tomorrow. It assumes that God expects us to store up for an emergency. But, if we put the kingdom first and our lives are aligned with it, Jesus promised to provide all that is needed. And, if the wealthier members of the body take their responsibilities seriously, the congregation is one of the means through which God provides.

The kingdom is the treasure hidden in the field, more valuable than anything the world can offer, and is of such absolute worth that we may sell or abandon all we have without ultimate loss.

It is a curious conceit on our part to expect the atonement of Messiah's death to cover over all the deliberate syncretism and apostasy that is the history and current state of the church—as if the church is immune to captivity because we are, after all, sinful people who have done the best we can. No doubt, it is pleasant and comforting to assume that, in the end, Messiah will graciously forgive all the syncretism, avarice, bloody violence, profligate horror, and persecution inflicted in his name, because those actions must be judged within the context of their time.[16] We are certain he will excuse our wanton worldliness because he understands our weakness and sinful nature and accepts us anyway.

But neither the Old nor New Testaments substantiates the idea of unconditional divine love toward man—even toward those who claim to follow him. We are obligated to constant watchfulness and repentance. We are to expel from our midst those who play-act and are unrepentant. Although atonement through Messiah provides abundant forgiveness, mercy, and love, he will not wink at individual or corporate sin in the church. To teach otherwise is apostasy. God's judgment begins in his ecclesia (1 Pet 4:17), and five of the letters to the seven churches in the Apocalypse describe the awful consequences of deliberately ignoring Messiah's repeated warnings to his people.

When Jesus asked if he would find "the faith" on the earth at his return (Luke 18:8), he meant an abiding trust in him that leads to selling all for the treasure in the field. He meant the faith that alters all aspects of life and, by its nature, places the disciple in conflict with surrounding

---

16. This is the "historian's excuse," which has the potential to justify *any* atrocity, since any action may be excused if refuge is taken within the context of the times or the personality of the individual.

society. His question was rhetorical, but the implied answer would appear to be "no."

The church has been in captivity since the end of the first century, and this explains both its dark history and its current state. Like Israel, the church has craved mammon and the things of the world, has comingled with them, and allowed them into the midst of the believing community—it has embraced them in the mistaken belief that syncretism is possible, or else that whatever is brought into the church is made holy thereby. Like Israel, the church has rejected the prophets and has grown in worldly power at the cost of its spiritual power.

One of the many lessons taught throughout Scripture is that deliberate and continued unfaithfulness results in captivity and exile. That principle applies equally to congregations and individuals. Yet, captivity has a purpose. God's judgments are never purely punitive. Captivity is a time when Jehovah reproves, tests, and attempts to mature his people. Just as he continued working amongst the Jews in captivity, so too the Holy Spirit is active today. The eternal ecclesia can never be defeated (Matt 16:18). God's plan is being accomplished, even while the church is directed by quislings. But, in captivity, the church is not in possession of those spiritual benefits and powers that were meant to abide in the ecclesia of Messiah.

In 1973, Os Guinness wrote that "the Christian community needs first to put its own house in order, to struggle to regain its integrity and clarity from its compromise with the present confusion."[17] Today, the institutional church is further from the mark than it was then. It has become more entangled in the things of the world, not less. During its captivity, it has defiled Jehovah's name in the presence of the nations, just as Israel did (Ezek 36:20-24).

The institutional church has always compromised readily and eagerly, and is paid handsomely for its accommodation. The donatives are generous and the arrangement is mutually beneficial to both parties. With power, money, and property, the church becomes an institution, like any other, and willingly nurtures its members into alignment with the expectations of the society where it exists—which is the function of any institution. As noted earlier, power and authority, once grasped, is seldom surrendered voluntarily.

---

17. Guinness, 365.

The parable of the wheat and tares (Matt 13:24–30) clearly teaches that the pure ecclesia does not exist. Until Jesus returns, the ecclesia will always contain those who resemble, but who are not, believers. One cannot remove them without peril to those who truly belong to the Lord. As Edersheim notes, the history of the church is strewn with remnants of unsuccessful attempts based on that flawed logic.[18] But the fact that the church can never be perfect does not grant its members permission to continue in stasis.

Although the institutional church is an edifice built in captivity, we cannot return to our inheritance by simply deciding to do so. The Jews did not determine when their captivity was complete. Jehovah initiated the return. We must also remember that not all Israel wanted to return. Some were content to stay where they were, in the houses they had built, surrounded by the comforts they had grown to love.

But for those who want restoration, we have a wonderful prophecy of promise and hope that Moses spoke of to Israel, even when he foresaw they would fall into apostasy and be exiled from the land:

> And it shall come to pass, when all these things are come upon thee . . . and thou shalt call them to mind among all the nations, whither Jehovah thy God hath driven thee, and shalt return unto Jehovah thy God, and shalt obey his voice according to all that I command thee this day, thou and thy children, with all thy heart, and with all thy soul; that then Jehovah thy God will turn thy captivity, and have compassion upon thee, and will return and gather thee from all the peoples, whither Jehovah thy God hath scattered thee. If *any of* thine outcasts be in the uttermost parts of heaven, from thence will Jehovah thy God gather thee, and from thence will he fetch thee: and Jehovah thy God will bring thee into the land which thy fathers possessed, and thou shalt possess it; and he will do thee good, and multiply thee above thy fathers. (Deut 30:1–5 ASV)

For those who truly desire restoration, our comfort lies in the trust that Messiah will bring the church back from captivity. He will do so to prove to the nations that he continues to love those who truly want to follow him—but it will not be the institution we knew. It will be the restored ecclesia.

---

18. Edersheim, 1:589–92.

In the meantime, we must measure ourselves against the Scriptures and against the lives of the first believers. We must seek truth over comfort. We must reject what does not align with the kingdom of God and its principles. We must examine whether we have imputed our own meaning to the descriptions in the New Testament of what our lives are supposed to be in Messiah. We must recognize our apostasy.

Irenaeus warned nineteen centuries ago that "lime is wickedly mixed with the milk of God."[19] Just so, we must ask Messiah to show us those areas in our lives where we have compromised or been led astray, or attempted to mix the unmixable. We must ask him to give us the desire to abandon comfortable Western ideas that we have mistaken for the truth. We must separate ourselves from the world, no matter the cost, just as the early believers did. We must be ready to sell all we have for the treasure in the field. We cannot serve God and mammon, and we cannot serve God and Caesar. We must turn away from those cherished, worldly embellishments and must yearn and pray for real and immediate direction by the Holy Spirit through the prophetic ministry.

This has been a long polemic, but it is justified by history and the lives of those early believers of the first century, who applied the teachings of Messiah Jesus willingly and joyfully with full knowledge of the cost.

The prophetic ministry is the chosen instrument through which the Holy Spirit leads the ecclesia, and we must earnestly pray for it to be restored to us. But we must also pray that the gift of discernment be lavished upon the body of Messiah, for it is discernment that permits us to continually question authority and doctrine. We must surrender human control and let Messiah build his ecclesia—to restore to us what he intended from the beginning. Just as he did for Israel, in his own time, at his command, he will restore the prophetic ministry and recall his ecclesia from captivity—for this is the very nature of the Almighty God and Messiah we serve: *ex malo bonum*.

---

19. Irenaeus, *Haer.* 3.17.4, ed. Roberts and Donaldson, 1:445.

Bibliography

The Apocrypha. New York: Thomas Nelson, 1894.
Arnold, Eberhard. *The Early Christians: In Their Own Words.* Rifton: Plough, 1972.
———. *Innerland: A Guide into the Heart of the Gospel.* Rifton: Plough, 1976.
———. *Salt and Light: Living the Sermon on the Mount.* Rifton: Plough, 1967.
Ball, W. E. *St. Paul and the Roman Law, and Other Studies in the Origin and Form of Doctrine.* Edinburgh: T&T Clark, 1901.
Beaty, James. *Paying the Pastor: Unscriptural and Traditional.* London: T. Fischer Unwin, 1885.
Belloc, Hilaire. *The Servile State.* London: T.N. Foulis, 1912.
Benson, Edward White. *Cyprian: His Life, His Times, His Work.* London: MacMillan, 1897.
Berkhof, Louis. *Systematic Theology.* Combined ed. Grand Rapids: Eerdmans, 1996.
Bigg, Charles. *The Origins of Christianity.* Edited by T. B. Strong. Oxford: Clarendon, 1909.
Bruce, F. F. *Paul: Apostle of the Heart Set Free.* Grand Rapids: Eerdmans, 1983. First published 1977 by Paternoster Press.
Bunsen, Christian Charles Josias. *Hippolytus and His Age: The Beginnings and Prospects of Christianity.* 2nd ed. 2 vols. London: Longman, Brown, Green & Longmans, 1854.
Dempsey, T. *The Delphic Oracle: Its Early History, Influence and Fall.* Oxford: B. H. Blackwell, 1918.
Dewey, John. *How We Think.* Boston: D. C. Heath and Company, 1933.
Deissmann, Adolf. *Light from the Ancient East: The New Testament Illustrated by Recently Discovered Texts of the Graeco-Roman World.* 2nd ed. Translated by Lionel R. M. Strachan. New York: Hodder & Stoughton, 1910.
Dobschutz, Ernst von. *The Apostolic Age.* Translated by F. L. Pogson. Boston: American Unitarian Association, 1910.
———. *Christian Life in the Primitive Church.* Translated by George Bremner. Edited by W. D. Morrison. London: Williams & Norgate, 1904.
Duchesne, Louis. *Early History of the Christian Church from its Foundation to the End of the Fifth Century.* 4th ed. 3 vols. New York: Longmans, Green, 1915.
Edersheim, Alfred. *The Life and Times of Jesus the Messiah.* 2 vols. 1886. Reprinted as a single volume, Grand Rapids: Eerdmans, 1977. Page references are to the 1886 edition.
Edmundson, George. *The Church in Rome in the First Century: An Examination of Various Controverted Questions Relating to its History, Chronology, Literature and Traditions.* London: Longmans, Green, 1913.
Faulkner, John Alfred. *Cyprian the Churchman.* Cincinnati: Jennings & Graham, 1906.
Fowler, W. Warde. *Social Life at Rome in the Age of Cicero.* New York: MacMillan, 1924.

Gibbon, Edward. *The Decline and Fall of the Roman Empire*. 2 vols. Great Books of the Western World, edited by Robert Maynard Hutchins, 40–41. Chicago: Encyclopaedia Britannica, 1952.

Gore, Charles. *The Church and the Ministry*. Edited by C. H. Turner. London: Longmans, Green, 1919.

———. *Orders and Unity*. New York: E. P. Dutton & Company, 1909.

Guinness, Os. *The Dust of Death: A Critique of the Establishment and the Counter Culture—and a Proposal for a Third Way*. Downers Grove: Inter-Varsity, 1973.

Harris, Helen B. *The Newly Recovered Apology of Aristides: Its Doctrine and Ethics*. Translated by J. Rendel Harris. London: Hodder & Stoughton, 1891.

Hatch, Edwin. *The Organization of the Early Christian Churches*. 2nd ed. London: Rivington, 1882.

Hitchcock, F. R. Montgomery. *Irenaeus of Lugdunum*. Cambridge: Cambridge University Press, 1914.

Hoppin, James M. *Pastoral Theology*. New York: Funk & Wagnalls, 1884.

Hort, Fenton John Anthony. *The Christian Ecclesia: A Course of Lectures on the Early History and Early Conceptions of the Ecclesia and Four Sermons*. London: MacMillan, 1897.

Illich, Ivan. *Deschooling Society*. Edited by Ruth Nanda Anshen. New York: Harper & Row, 1970.

Innes, A. Taylor. *The Trial of Jesus Christ: A Legal Monograph*. Edinburgh: T&T Clark, 1899.

Kaye, John. *The Ecclesiastical History of the Second and Third Centuries as Illustrated from the Writings of Tertullian*. 3rd ed. London: Francis & Rivington, 1845.

Keating, J. F. *The Agape and the Eucharist in the Early Church*. London: Methuen, 1901.

Lewis, John Delaware. *The Letters of the Younger Pliny*. London: Kegan Paul, Trench, Trübner, 1890.

Lightfoot, J. B. *The Apostolic Fathers*. Edited by J. R. Harmer. London: McMillan, 1912.

———. *The Christian Ministry*. London: MacMillan, 1901.

Lindsay, Thomas M. *The Church and the Ministry in the Early Centuries*. 2nd ed. London: Hodder & Stoughton, 1903.

Lowrie, Walter. *The Church and Its Organization in Primitive and Catholic Times*. London: Longmans, Green, 1904.

———. *Problems of Church Unity*. London: Longmans, Green, 1924.

MacLeod, Norman. *Church, Ministry, and Sacraments*. London: A&C Black, 1898.

MacMullen, Ramsay. *Paganism in the Roman Empire*. New Haven: Yale University, 1981.

Moxom, Philip Stafford. *From Jerusalem to Nicea: The Church in the First Three Centuries*. Boston: Roberts Brothers, 1896.

Orr, James. *The History and Literature of the Early Church*. London: Hodder & Stoughton, 1913.

Pullan, Leighton. *Early Christian Doctrine*. London: Rivington, 1899.

Ramsay, W. M. *The Church in the Roman Empire before A.D. 170*. New York: G. P. Putnam's Sons, 1893.

Roberts, Alexander and James Donaldson, eds. *The Ante-Nicene Fathers: Translations of the Writings of the Fathers down to 325*. 10 vols. New York: Scribner's, 1913.

Robertson, A. T. *Luke the Historian in Light of Historical Research*. New York: Scribner's, 1920.

Robinson, John A. T. *Redating the New Testament*. London: SCM Press, 1976.

Salomon, Louis B. *Semantics and Common Sense*. New York: Holt, Rinehart & Winston, 1966.
Sanday, W. *The Conception of the Priesthood in the Early Church and in the Church of England*. 2nd ed. London: Longmans, Green, 1899.
Schaff, Philip. *History of the Christian Church*. 3rd revision. 7 vols. New York: Charles Scribner's Sons, 1889.
———. *The Oldest Church Manual Called the Teaching of the Twelve Apostles*. New York: Charles Scribner's Sons, 1885.
Schodde, George H. *The Book of Enoch: Translated from the Ethiopic with Introduction and Notes*. Andover: Warren F. Draper, 1882.
Selwyn, Edward Carus. *The Christian Prophets and the Prophetic Apocalypse*. London: MacMillan, 1900.
———. *St. Luke the Prophet*. London: MacMillan, 1901.
Simcox, William Henry. *The Beginnings of the Christian Church*. London: Rivington, 1881.
Snyder, Howard A. *The Problem of Wineskins*. Downers Grove: Inter-Varsity, 1975.
Swete, Henry Barclay. *The Holy Spirit in the New Testament: A Study of Primitive Christian Teaching*. London: MacMillan, 1921.
Tacitus, P. Cornelius. *The Annals*. Translated by Alfred John Church and William Jackson Brodribb. Great Books of the Western World, edited by Robert Maynard Hutchins, 15. Chicago: Encyclopædia Britannica, 1952.
Trench, Richard C. *A Select Glossary of English Words Used Formerly in Senses Different from Their Present*. London: George Routledge & Sons, 1906.
Weizsacker, Carl von. *The Apostolic Age of the Christian Church*. 2nd ed. 2 vols. Translated by James Millar. London: Williams & Norgate, 1897.
Wotherspoon, H. J. *The Ministry in the Church in Relation to Prophecy and Spiritual Gifts (Charismata)*. London: Longmans, Green, 1916.

Subject/Name Index

A

abortion, 45
accommodation to paganism, 49, 70, 71, 86, 92, 132
acolytes. *See* lower orders
Agabus, 16, 20, 103, 104
Agape, 26–27, 117
    abandonment of, 82, 118
ambassadors for Christ, 43
anonymous accusers. *See delatores*
antistes, 82
Apocalypse, *See* Revelation
    apocalypses, 22, 115, 117
apostasy, 50, 54, 123, 127, 131, 133–34
    as goal of magistrate, 80
    apostles
    and apocalypses, 15
    and ecclesia, 6, 8, 10, 11
    and elders, 15
    and form of ecclesia, 6, 8, 10, 11, 28
    and paid pastorate, 126
    and prophets, 6, 13, 20, 22, 25, 28, 115, 117
    as bishops, 83
    as minister of worship, 55
    as officers, 110
    as prophet, 14–15
    as prophetic ministry, 13, 15
    cited as Scripture by, 17
    Didache and, 25
    displaced, eclipsed, 115, 118, 124
    distinction between prophet and, 13–15
    double function of, 21
    guided by Holy Spirit, 16
    Ignatius on, 66–68
    last surviving, 95
    memoirs of, 23
    original, 28, 59, 69, 118
    Peter as chief, 3, 105
    prophets and teachers, 13, 55
    second ordinances of, 65
    the Twelve, 88, 102
    translation of word, 13
    used to confirm, 109
    wandering, 14–15, 20
    work of, 15
apostolic succession
    and the episcopacy, 94, 96, 98–105, 107
    idea of, 64–66, 68–71, 94, 118, 119
apostolic tradition, 105
Apostolic Traditions, 45, 71
appointed, 83, 91, 101, 128
    in ecclesia(e), 9, 65, 83, 91, 102, 103
    term used by Paul, 10
argument from silence, 109, 111
argument from tradition, 98
Aristides, 36
Arnold, Eberhard, 23, 29, 50, 129, 130
asceticism, 92
assembly, 3, 4, 6, 28, 71, 126
authority,
    as characteristic of the ecclesia, 5, 7, 108
    power and, 119, 132
    transfer of, 102

B

Ball, W. E., 17–19, 68
baptism, 62, 72, 86, 88, 101, 103, 120
    as sacred event, 27
    barred from, 45, 76

140 Subject/Name Index

baptism - continued
   gifts bestowed at, 86, 118
   infant, 127
Beaty, James, 119, 120, 126
behavior. See Christian life, behavior
Benson, Edward, 78, 79–81, 83–84
Berkhof, Louis, 44
Bigg, Charles, 40–43, 58–60
binding and loosing (keys), 5, 68, 127
bishops
   as center of church, 66–69
   as defender of faith, 72
   as priest, 82–84
   Cyprian's idea of, 3, 62, 69, 76–77, 81–87, 104–5
   defined as the church, 62, 118
   election of, 62, 64, 75, 85
   elevated above elders, 56, 60, 61, 62, 64–71, 72
   executed, 81
   interchangeable with presbyter, 56
   occupations, 77
   origin of, 8
Bruce, F. F., 44
burial societies, 10, 78, 80
business meeting. See ecclesia, meetings

C

Callistus, 81, 87
Canons of Hippolytus, 82, 86
captivity and exile, 122, 132
caste, 27, 84, 105, 118, 125
catholic. See church
Catholics, 127, 128
celibacy, 92
Celsus, 18, 33, 34, 39, 43, 85
certificate of good standing, 89
certificates of exemption *(libelli)*, 74, 81
   false, 73
charismatic ministry, 21, 95
charity. See poor, care of
Christian life
   and behavior, 25, 26, 31, 32, 46, 105, 129
   as list of rules, 29
   description of, 29–53
   early, 29–53
   safety net principle and, 131

   sharing of wealth, 10, 27, 32, 35, 57, 129
   the Law and, 29–33
Christianity
   as revolution, 48–49
   becomes state religion, 54
   primitive, 3
Christians
   and government, 41, 43, 128, 134
   and separation from society, 39–40
   and surrounding society, 33, 42, 119
   and the military, 43
   as a scandal, 39
   cheesecake, 126
   heresy and persecution, 54, 104, 118
   magistrate and, 40, 50, 78–80
   pagan beliefs about, 38–39
   persecution of, 28, 53, 54, 62, 63, 70, 72–73, 75, 77, 78, 79–81, 88, 92, 104, 118, 131
   prohibited occupations, 45
   suspicion of, 41, 52, 78–79
Chrysostom, 115–16
church
   adaptation by, 106, 112, 120
   apostasy in, 33, 54, 123, 127, 131
   catholic, 11, 58, 60, 68, 74, 76, 91, 93, 100, 119, 127, 128
   Cyprian and, 82–84
   defined as presence of bishop, 62, 118
   derivation of word, 2
   disorder in, 63
   early, 1, 2, 3, 18, 57, 66, 114, 123
   Imperial, 87–93
   in captivity, 122, 123, 131, 132–34
   institutional, 2, 3, 7, 8, 33, 54, 81, 93, 99, 100, 106, 119, 122, 124–27, 132–33
   meaning of word today, 2–3
   meetings. See ecclesia, meetings
   membership, 6–7
   ministry of tables in, 9, 13
   officers, 10, 12, 23, 28, 55, 61, 62, 90, 97, 100, 102, 106, 110, 123, 124
   pagans and, 30, 71, 92, 118

prophecy in, 18, 21, 27, 55–57, 60–61, 95, 102, 108, 110
Roman, 65
today, 7, 109, 120, 123–127
two conceptions of, 100
universal, 67, 72, 106
Church of Christ, 11, 14, 70, 93
Clement of Alexandria, 18, 70
Clement of Rome, 55, 62, 64, 65, 83, 95
clergy, 22, 24, 64, 69, 75, 93, 118–19, 121, 125–27
and salaries. *See* salaries
as caste or class, 90–92, 105, 106, 107, 122
origin of, 84, 90
clergy-laity division, 84, 86, 107, 118, 119, 126
client-patron relationship, 9, 38
as model for ecclesia, 10
collegiae, 9, 10, 38
illicit, 11
commission, 13, 14, 98, 101–4, 107
common meal, 10, 23, 26, 82
communal living, 128
communion, 81
of saints, 105–6
those barred from, 46, 73, 76, 87
conflict
where none exists, 22
with the world, 29, 131
between James and Paul, 31
with faith, 47, 118, 120
with the Holy Spirit, 124
of power, 74
confraternities, 9–11, 26, 27, 38, 48
as model for ecclesia, 10
congregations
discernment in, 13, 20–21, 24, 25, 27, 117
Gentile, 20, 56, 95
independence of, 6–7, 11, 85, 125
of God, 4
organization of, 7–13, 96–97, 107, 117
segregation in, 86
connotation, 1–2

Constantine, Emperor, 60, 87–89, 91, 121
converts, 14, 33–34, 36, 58, 69, 86
pagan, 70, 118
Jewish, 11, 30
Cornelius, bishop of Rome, 85
Cornelius, centurion, 103
Council
of Arles, 89
of Constantinople, 60
of Laodicea, 82
of Paris, 86
cult of the emperor. *See* imperial cult
Cyprian, 3, 61, 62, 69, 75–77, 81–82, 84, 87, 104, 105
deacons, 9, 20, 22, 23, 26, 28, 52, 61, 66, 67, 81, 84, 86, 90, 110, 117, 118
ministry of tables, 13
dead letter, 44

D

Decian persecution, 72–73, 77, 80–81
Decius, Emperor, 72, 77, 81
Deissmann, Adolf, 43, 49, 111,
delatores, 53, 79
Delphic Oracle, 12
Dempsey, T., 12
denotation, 1–2
deuterocanonical writings, 17, 23, 44
Dewey, John, 120
Didache
and discernment, 25
and prophetic ministry, 21–22, 25, 55, 57, 63, 97
and the Two Ways, 43, 45
estimated date of writing, 24
extracts from, 25, 43, 45–46
discernment
complement to prophecy, 21
definition of gift, 20
gift of, 24, 25, 27, 63, 98, 104, 134
disciples, 3, 4, 34, 54, 98, 105, 113–15, 129
discipleship, 25

Subject/Name Index

discipline, 59, 72, 76, 77, 80, 85, 118, 125, 126
divine presence, 27, 108, 109, 111, 115, 116, 122, 126
Dobschutz, Ernst von, 46, 64,
doctrine
    false, 13, 54, 63, 124
    illegitimate transfer of, 3
    protected by creed, 71
    unity of, 85
Domitian, Emperor, 9, 95
Duchesne, Louis, 57–58, 88–89
    early Christians, 3, 33, 42, 46, 117, 119
    as viewed by pagans, 34

E

ecclesia
    adaptation of organizations by, 8, 10, 11, 72, 85
    and poor members, 35–36
    and secular associations, 8
    as called out, 4
    as ideal, 5, 7, 72
    as theocracy, 6
    as tiny island, 7, 117
    as understood by Jew and Gentile, 4
    as used by Jesus, 3
    classes of use in NT, 5–6
    conflicts among members, 27
    definition changes, 71–72
    discussion of, 1–7
    five characteristics of, 5
    five models of, 8–9
    in homes, 34
    Jesus' presence in, 27, 67, 108, 109, 115, 116
    local and independent, 6, 12
    local ministry in, 27
    meetings, 23–27
    membership, 6–7
    no imposition of form, 11–12
    of Israel, 6
    of Messiah, 4
    Paul's idea of, 4, 6–7, 10,
    spiritual gifts in, 27
    universal, 5–7. *See also* church, universal
    upper and lower classes in, 33–34
    what it is not, 6
ecclesiastical
    authority, 28, 98
    government, 64, 69, 96, 107
    models, 9–11
    organization, 9, 90, 94, 97, 98
    structure, 98
Edersheim, Alfred, 98, 111, 124, 130, 133
Edict of Milan, 87, 91
edification, 23, 27, 105, 117, 119
Edmundson, George, 95
elders
    collegiate session of, 61, 64, 117, 118
    elected by popular vote, 10
    in the ecclesia, 6, 9, 13, 15, 22, 23, 26, 27, 28, 54, 56, 62, 72, 73, 74, 86, 90, 98, 102
    veneration of Jewish, 66
Enoch
    book of, 18, 59
    used by prophets, 17–18
episcopacy
    and apostolic succession, 64–71, 94, 96, 98, 104–5, 107, 118, 119
    appearance and growth of, 60–61, 94–96
    defense of, 96–106
    definition of, 64
Eucharist, 26, 60, 67, 73, 82, 83, 85, 118
excommunication, 33, 89, 93
exile, 122, 132, 133
exorcists. *See* lower orders expropriation, 19, 86, 125
extra ecclesium nulla salus, 92, 101, 107

F

faith
    as basis of ecclesia, 5
    Christian, 3–4, 30, 37, 65
    denial of, 53, 72, 73, 80
    expression of, 31, 33, 35,

in Messiah, 11, 29, 129
individual, 99
Jesus and, 113–14, 131
new, 37–38
profession of, 43, 117
rule of, 16, 71
transmission of, 23
true, 117, 129, 131
without works, 31, 36
false prophet. *See* prophets
fasting, 103
Faulkner, John, 75, 76, 77, 78, 81
feasts and fasts, 92
finance officer, 8
Fowler, W. Warde, 26
fulfillment
    primary and secondary, 18

G

genius. *See* imperial cult
gentiles, 4, 11, 33
    as converts, 30, 31
    Law and, 30–31
genus tertium, 42, 78
Gibbon, Edward, 41, 47, 49, 88, 91, 94121
gifts
    administrative, 110
    bestowed by bishop, 86
    cessation of, 61, 104, 108–16
    normal, 110
    spiritual gifts, 27, 110, 127
    supernatural, 94, 104, 108–16
    tongues, 108, 110
God
    Invisible, 35, 39
    serve, 35, 114, 134
    kingdom of, 32, 38, 43, 70, 101, 106, 114, 134
    people of, 4
    will of, 19, 21, 77
    Word of, 14, 57–59
gods, 4, 26, 37, 38, 40, 41, 43, 48, 49, 51, 52, 54, 58
Gore, Charles, 60, 61, 63,
    on the episcopacy, 55–56, 96–106,
    on gifts, 109–11
    on prophets, 15–16
Guinness, Os, 132

H

Hatch, Edwin, 2, 3, 8, 23, 90, 92, 97, 105, 106
haters of mankind. *See odium generis humani*
heresy, 20, 59, 61, 63, 70, 83, 89–91, 124
heretics, 68, 72, 89–91
hermeneutics, 18
hierarchy, 7, 55, 107, 125, 126
Hitchcock, Montgomery, 67–68
Holy Spirit, 6, 11, 19, 24, 29, 30, 32, 33, 54, 85, 103, 104, 118, 128, 132
    direction by, 13, 16, 20, 45, 57, 59, 63, 124, 126, 134
    in life of believer, 29, 30–33
homosexuality, 32
hospitality, 46
Hoppin, James, 115
Hort, Fenton, 2–6, 31, 35, 106

I

Ignatius, 55, 56, 61, 62, 64, 66, 72
Illich, Ivan, 124–25
imperial cult, 42, 49–50, 118
    church adopts, 84–85
Ingersoll, Robert, 91
Innes, A. Taylor, 37–38
innovation in religion. *See* religion
institutional church. *See* church
institutionalism, 124
institutions
    characteristics of, 124
    pagan, 8, 85
intermediaries, 107, 126
Irenaeus, 17, 18, 55, 61, 64, 65–67, 68, 71, 95, 114, 134
Israel, 4, 5, 6, 13, 19, 66, 83, 116, 121, 122, 123, 126, 132, 133, 134

J

Jerome, 62
Jerusalem Council, 31
Jerusalem congregation, 9
Jew and Gentile, 30–31
Judaism, 11, 44, 48, 66, 76, 125
Judaizers, 31
Judgment
    by Christians, 18, 44, 47, 75, 117, 128
    by fire, 47
    by Roman authorities, 51, 78
    God's, 18, 25, 44, 128, 131–32
    in the ecclesia, 7, 22, 25, 61
    of prophets, 22, 25
    wrath and, 44, 117, 128
Julian, Emperor, 12, 121–22
jury, 128
Justin Martyr, 17, 23, 36

K

Kaye, John, 91
Keating, J. F., 26, 36, 38, 82
keys. *See* binding and loosing

L

labarum, 89
laity. *See* clergy-laity division
lapsed *(lapsi)*, 53, 72–74, 81, 83, 85, 87
lauds and vespers, 92
law and grace, 44
lawyers, 69, 70
laying on of hands, 66, 86, 102, 103, 118
leadership, 11, 12, 13, 28, 56, 61, 102, 118, 125
legal fiction, 69, 84, 124
leges maiestatis, 79
Lenten vows, 92
Letter to Trajan, 50–52
Levites, 83, 127
Lewis, John, 50–52
libelli, See certificates of exemption
Lightfoot, J. B., 56, 62, 70, 83, 95, 97, 107

Lindsay, Thomas, 21, 23, 27, 29, 35, 61, 62, 64, 82, 84, 90, 105, 108, 114
    on apostolic succession, 65, 68–69
    on lawyers, 69
    on ecclesia, 3–15
living Word, 44
local ministry
    and prophetic ministry, 13, 20, 22, 28, 55, 61, 63, 64
    collegiate, 23, 27
    democratically chosen, 22
    members of, 22
    not salaried, 22, 26, 28, 119
    task of, 22–23
    threefold, 61–62, 84
Lord's Supper. *See* Agape
lower orders, 84
Lowrie, Walter, 3–4, 7, 95–96, 105

M

MacLeod, Norman, 72, 84
MacMullen, Ramsay, 26
magistrate, 40, 50, 78–80, 89, 90
    barred as Christian occupation, 45
mammon, 122, 128, 130, 132, 134
Mariolatry, 92
martyrs
    power of, 73, 74, 78, 81
    struggle by bishops against, 82, 93, 118
meaning
    illegitimate transfer of, 3, 33
    words and, 1–3
meat sacrificed to idols, 26
meetings at night, 36
Messiah, 5, 11, 19, 26, 29, 30, 31, 32, 63, 115, 122, 124, 126–29, 131–34
    Ecclesia of, 4, 5, 7, 13, 132
Milvian Bridge, 89
ministry of the tables, 13
ministry of the Word, 13, 99
Minucius Felix, 38
miracles, 102, 108, 109, 112–15
miraculous
    Jesus and, 112–15

Subject/Name Index   145

redefining of, 113
  withdrawal of, 104, 109–15
  withheld, 111
miraculous gifts. *See* gifts
money, 9, 25, 36, 77, 90, 91, 115, 126, 128, 129, 130, 132
Montanism, 56–58, 61, 70, 91, 92, 95
  declared heresy, 59–60
Moses, 29, 32, 83, 126, 133
Moxom, Philip, 56, 123

N

Nero, 33, 47–48
normal gifts. *See* gifts
Novatian, 85–86

O

occupations, 32, 46, 50, 76, 117, 128
  bishops and, 77
  local ministry and, 26
  prohibited, 45, 70, 71, 128
odium generis humani, 42, 48
ordain. *See* ordination
orders. *See* lower orders
ordination, 24, 83, 94, 96, 98, 101, 102, 106, 107, 119, 120, 122, 126, 127
  and apostolic succession, 83, 100, 104
  as confirmation, 103–4
  as segregation, 124–25
  authority for, 103–4
  direct no longer possible, 104
  in Roman law, 68
Origen, 17, 18, 34, 39, 43
Orr, James, 49
orthodoxy, 55, 64, 89, 93
overseers, 8, 23

P

paganism, 40–44
  and Christians, 40–53
  Christian accommodation of, 49, 70, 71, 86, 92, 132
  prophecy in, 12
papacy, 69, 82, 94, 98
parable, 130, 133
Paraclete, 57–58
paid pastorate. *See* salaries
pastor, 13, 21, 22, 23, 26, 27, 28, 58, 86, 90, 101, 126, 127
  and salaries. *See* salaries
Paul
  address at Miletus, 4, 6, 54, 90
  and apostasy, 54
  and prophetic ministry, 13, 15–16, 20, 22
  and gifts, 108, 111, 115
  writing to the ecclesiae, 23
persecution
  Decian, 72–73, 79–81
  end of Christian, 88, 92, 118
Peter, 3–4, 5, 16, 19, 20, 47, 73, 102, 103, 105, 113, 127
plebs and *ordo*, 86
Pliny Secundus, 11, 50, 52, 53, 80
  his Letter to Trajan, 50–52
Plutarch, 12
politics, 41, 42, 48
Pontifex Maximus, 82
poor
  as viewed by Romans, 36
  care of by ecclesia, 26, 35, 36
possessions, 32, 130
presbyters, 55, 56, 62, 65–68, 75, 81, 83, 84, 92, 110, 126
priest
  definition of, 83
  in the church, 71, 83, 84, 126
priesthood, 13, 82–84, 90, 122
prophecy
  as teaching of the bishop, 61
  Christian, 12, 16, 18, 19, 21, 22, 27, 47, 56–57, 59–60, 63, 65, 95, 108, 110
  false, 104, 129
  pagan, 12
  withdrawn, 56, 61, 104, 109–15

prophetic ministry
    and local ministry, 13
    as unpredictable, 63, 124, 127
    eclipse of, 22, 55, 56, 61, 64, 93, 94, 95, 97, 115, 118, 119, 120, 123
    how commissioned, 13, 14, 104
    leadership of the, 12–16
    Paul and, 13, 15–16, 20, 22, 24, 102
    purpose of, 6, 12–13, 55, 63, 117, 122, 123, 134
    restrictions on, 55, 56, 61, 71, 95, 124
prophets
    and disorder, 63
    become apostles, 15
    conscious activity of, 15
    ecstasy, 16
    false, 19, 20, 25, 55, 59, 60, 63
    foretelling, 16
    interpretation of Scripture, 18
    Montanist, 57
    as nucleus of ecclesia, 13
    test of, 20, 25, 62, 67, 98, 104
    use of Scripture, 16–19
    wandering, 15
    distinguished from apostles, 13–15
    in *Didache*, 25
proselytize, 37, 76
Protestant Reformation, 127
providential safeguard, 70, 72, 96, 97, 104

R

Rabbi, rabbinic, 5, 31, 98, 127
Radical Reformers, 42, 45, 127, 128
Ramsay, W.M., 37, 40, 48–49,
readers. *See* lower orders
relics, 92
religio licita, 11, 76, 78
religion
    innovation in, 37, 40, 87
    in Roman empire, 10, 11, 36, 49, 73, 75, 76, 80, 86, 88, 89, 92, 119
responsibility, 9, 25, 62
individual, 63, 84, 98, 126
restoration, 27, 73, 74, 127, 129, 133

restoration of all things, 7, 47
retribution, 32, 42, 44
Revelation, 4, 19, 109, 131
    date of, 95
revelation, 19, 20, 55
Rex Legia, 79
rich, the, 34, 36, 129
riches, 91
Riedemann, Peter, 127
Robinson, John, 95
Roman law, 41
    applied to the church polity, 68–69, 86
Rome
    church in, 84, 87
    Great Fire of, 47–48

S

sacrifice
    Christian life as, 5, 32, 83
    Eucharist as, 82–84, 118
    pagan, 26, 43, 89
    to emperor, 50, 79
saints
    Christians as, 70, 71, 105
    worship of, 92
salaries (stipends), 22, 26, 28, 90, 91, 119, 120
salvation
    and hospitality, 46
    and the church, 87, 92–93, 106, 119
    as process of growth, 32
    Cyprian and, 77
    description of, 30–33
    evidence of, 31–33, 46, 127, 129
    Gore and, 99, 101
    outside the church, 73, 87, 92–93, 101, 106, 119
Sanday, W., 65–66
Satyricon, 33
Schaff, Philip, 24–25, 44, 48, 88
Scripture
    Montanism and, 58–59
    four uses by prophets, 17
    private interpretation of, 19
    its use by prophets, 16–19

second ordinances, 65
secrecy, 36, 38, 39, 78, 79, 80
secular associations, 8, 10
Selwyn, Edward, 13, 14–20, 22, 24, 30, 61–63, 66, 91
semantics, 1–2
sensus plenior, 18
Sermon on the Mount, 31
service of tables, 9
Severus, Emperor, 76
shrines, 92
Simcox, William, 36
Simons, Meno, 127
sins and forgiveness, 73, 87
slaves, conversion of, 46
Snyder, Howard, 122
sojourner, 32, 70
soldiers, 45, 79, 89
special gifts. *See* gifts
stewards, 84, 101, 102
supernatural gifts. *See* gifts
suspect, 119, 125, 127
sword, 42, 45, 60, 89, 93, 121, 127, 130
synagogue, 2, 9, 11, 66
syncretism, 33, 70, 71, 77, 92, 119, 120, 122, 125, 131, 132

T

Tacitus, 33, 47–48
Teachers, 13, 20, 22, 71, 103, 110
teaching, 20, 23, 25, 30, 44, 47, 55, 57, 58, 59, 60, 61, 64, 71, 76, 95, 96, 105, 110, 134
  authoritative, 98, 125
  hard, 129, 130
  traditional, 35, 98
Tertullian, 10, 17, 56, 65, 67–69, 71, 73, 82, 84, 87, 91
  and Montanism, 57, 58
test by Roman authorities, 50, 53, 79
testing of prophets. *See* prophets
the Seven, 9
theocracy, 5, 6, 7
Theodosius, Emperor, 12, 54, 60, 89
third race. *See genus tertium*

toleration, religious, 37–38, 70, 86, 89, 91, 121
tongues. *See* gifts
torture, 48, 52, 53, 73, 79, 80, 81
tradition, 11, 57, 63, 64, 68, 98, 99, 107, 126
Trajan, Emperor, 9, 50–53, 80
treason, 79
trust, 32, 44, 114, 115, 128, 131, 133
Twelve, the, 4, 5, 13, 63, 83, 101, 102, 106, 115
Two Ways, the, 43–45, 117, 120, 127
  and Calvinism, 44
twofold ministry, 13, 21, 22, 25, 55, 61, 117

U

universal church. *See* church

V

Vespasian, Emperor, 95
vestments, 84

W

war, 121, 127, 130
wealth
  as gift from God, 35, 117
  as obstacle, 70
  dangers of, 128–30
  sharing. *See* Christian life
  use of, 10, 32, 35–36, 117, 129, 131
Weizsacker, Carl von, 34, 35
women, 27, 38, 57, 70
  as prophets, 20
  Cyprian and, 76–77
worry, 32
Wotherspoon, H. J., 21–22, 24, 100, 111–12
wrath, 32, 42, 44, 54, 117, 127, 128

www.ingramcontent.com/pod-product-compliance
Lightning Source LLC
Chambersburg PA
CBHW051108160426
43193CB00010B/1361